Adam Temple is a barrister at 4 Pump Court, specialising in financial services law. He regularly appears for the Financial Conduct Authority in regulatory cases, and for banks, IFAs and insurance companies in all manner of disputes. He has particular expertise in FOS claims and is regularly instructed to advise on matters of systemic interest to his clients. He has appeared for an Interested Party in a judicial review of a FOS decision.

Robert Scrivener is a barrister at 4 Pump Court. He routinely acts in banking and financial services disputes, particularly appearing for insurers, banks and other authorised firms. He has been instructed on a number of cases arising from FOS decisions, and is often instructed in disputes giving rise to issues under the Financial Services and Markets Act and the FCA Handbook.

A Practical Guide to Financial Ombudsman Service Claims

A Practical Guide to Financial Ombudsman Service Claims

Adam Temple
MA, BCL (Oxon)
Barrister, 4 Pump Court

Robert Scrivener
BA (Cantab)
Barrister, 4 Pump Court

Law Brief Publishing

Published 2018 by Law Brief Publishing, an imprint of Law Brief Publishing Ltd
30 The Parks
Minehead
Somerset
TA24 8BT

www.lawbriefpublishing.com

Paperback: 978-1-911035-66-4

LIST OF SOURCES

Wade & Forsyth's *Administrative Law* (11th Ed., OUP) p. 70

http://www.ombudsman-decisions.org.uk

http://www.fnancial-ombudsman.org.uk

https://www.fca.org.uk/publication/mou/mou-fos.pdf

http://www.financial-ombudsman.org.uk/consumer/complaints.htm

https://register.fca.org.uk

FCA's letter to LMA dated 17 July 2014 (available at http://www.citysolicitors.org.uk/attachments/article/121/20140820%20Letter%20from%20FCA%20regarding%20implications%20of%20decision%20in%20matter%20of%20Fons%20HF%20(in%20liquidation)%20v%20Corporal%20Limited%20and%20Pillar%20Securitisation%20S%20a%20r%20l.pdf)

http://www.financial-ombudsman.org.uk/faq/businesses/vj.html

http://www.financial-ombudsman.org.uk/publications/pdf/Micro-enterprise-complaints-Aug-2015.pdf

FCA CP 18/3, January 2018: 'Consultation on SME access to the Financial Ombudsman Service and Feedback to DP15/7: SMEs as Users of Financial Services' (available at https://www.fca.org.uk/publications/consultation-papers/cp18-3-consultation-sme-access-financial-ombudsman-service)

http://www.financial-ombudsman.org.uk/publications/technical_notes/six-month-time-limit.htm#10

http://www.financial-ombudsman.org/publications/consumer-leaflet.htm

http://www.financial-ombudsman.org/publications/ombudsman-news/94/94.pdf

http://www.financial-ombudsman.org.uk/publications/factsheets/what-happen-now-my-case-has-been-referred-to-an-ombudsman.pdf

http://www.financial-ombudsman.org.uk/publications/technical_notes/QG-ombudsman-panel.pdf

http://www.financial-ombudsman.org.uk/about/panel-ombudsmen.html

https://ico.org.uk/media/action-weve-taken/decision-notices/2014/1008586/fs_50500980.pdf

https://ec.europa.eu/consumers/odr/main/?event=main.adr.show2

http://www.financial-ombudsman.org.uk/faq/pdf/Equitable_Penrose-related_decision.pdf

http://www.financial-ombudsman.org.uk/assets/pdf/2017-12-01-MoU-between-The%20Pensions-Ombudsman-and-the-Financial-Ombudsman-Service.pdf

http://www.financial-ombudsman.org.uk/publications/technical_notes/QG3-hearings.pdf

http://www.financial-ombudsman.org/publications/technical_notes/compensation-for-investment-loss.htm

http://www.financial-ombudsman.org/publications/technical_notes/compensation-for-investment-loss.htm

http://www.financial-ombudsman.org/publications/technical_notes/calculating-comp-investment-complaint.html

http://www.financial-ombudsman.org/publications/technical_notes/distress-and-inconvenience.htm

http://www.financial-ombudsman.org.uk/publications/technical_notes/compensation.html

http://www.financial-ombudsman.org.uk/publications/ombudsman-news/33/awards-33.htm

Final Notices for Glyn Goodyear dated 14 April 2016 (https://www.fca.org.uk/publication/final-notices/glyn-goodyear.pdf) and for Foreman Financial Services Limited dated 23 October 2017 (https://www.fca.org.uk/publication/final-notices/foreman-financial-services-ltd-2017.pdf)

PREFACE

The aim of this book is to provide a high level guide to disputes before the Financial Ombudsman Service (or 'FOS'). We also look at how FOS decisions interact with litigation and how to challenge FOS decisions when unhappy with them.

One of the most important parts of financial services regulation is a guarantee that the clients of those who provide such services are able to complain and seek redress. For many such clients, the FOS represents an efficient and cost effective means enabling them to do just that. In those cases which are not finally resolved by the FOS, the FOS proceedings will often represent the first step in a lengthier dispute which may not be resolved until a court finally gives judgment.

Whilst many FOS claims will not involve lawyers, our experience is that legal advisors often assist parties before the FOS (particularly on the respondent side, given their size or the availability of indemnity insurance). It seemed to us that, in light of this, there might be some use for a short book outlining the key parts of FOS procedure.

Given its complexity, we have not attempted to go into the full detail of the FCA Handbook's DISP chapter. Instead, we have tried to write what we hope is a helpful guide which will either enable the reader to find the answer to the main points about how FOS claims work, or at least be pointed in the right direction for more niche issues.

Anyone familiar with financial services regulation will know how frequently the regulator likes to update its rules. With that in mind, we have tried to state the law as at 13 January 2018. Whilst finalising the proofs of this book, however, we received a transcript of the Administrative Court's decision in *R (Kelly) v FOS* [2017] EWHC 3581 (Admin). Whilst it was a successful challenge to a FOS decision on the grounds of procedural error, failure to apply the correct test and also irrationality, we do not consider that the case creates new law. It has not, therefore, been incorporated into the text.

Adam Temple & Robert Scrivener
March 2018

CONTENTS

TABLE OF ABBREVIATIONS AND COMMONLY USED TERMS

This book uses a number of abbreviations throughout, as set out below:

DISP	The 'Dispute Resolution: Complaints' section of the Financial Conduct Authority's Handbook
CRD	Capital Requirements Directive
CBTL	Consumer buy-to-let
FCA	Financial Conduct Authority
FOS	Financial Ombudsman Service
FSA	Financial Services Authority (the previous name of the Financial Conduct Authority)
FSMA	Financial Services and Markets Act 2000
Glossary	Glossary of the Financial Conduct Authority's Handbook
Handbook	The Rules and Guidance promulgated by the Financial Conduct Authority.
MiFID	Markets in Financial Instruments Directive
RAO	Financial Services and Markets Act 2000 (Regulated Activities) Order 2001

TABLE OF CASES

TABLE OF LEGISLATION

TABLE OF FCA HANDBOOK PROVISIONS

CHAPTER ONE INTRODUCTION TO THE FOS

This book is about the Financial Ombudsman Service (or 'FOS'). The FOS is probably the main form of alternative dispute resolution for customers of those who are subject to financial regulation. In this way it provides an important way of resolving a wide variety of claims and complaints.

The purpose of this book is to look at the principal issues that arise when the FOS is asked to determine a complaint, as well as touch on how the FOS relates to other dispute resolution procedures, most notably litigation.

The history of the FOS

The concept of an ombudsman first appeared in Scandinavian countries. Sweden has had some form of ombudsman for over one hundred and fifty years.[1] But it was not until the Parliamentary Commissioner Act 1967 that the institution first made its way to Britain. The purpose of that commission was to provide a method of investigating and remedying complaints about central government that were brought through members of the House of Commons. Over time, its role expanded. Complaints can now be brought by members of the public, and it is today called the Parliamentary and Health Service Ombudsman. It allows complaints to be made against a wide array of government departments and services, as well as the NHS.

Since the first ombudsman in 1967, there have been a number of ombudsman spring up to regulate other industries. Many – such as the Legal Services Ombudsman and the Housing Ombudsman – have statutory bases. Others are purely voluntary.

---

1 Wade & Forsyth's *Administrative Law* (11th Ed., OUP) p. 70.

The FOS falls into the former category, though as will be seen many organisations sign up to its so-called 'voluntary jurisdiction' and would otherwise fall outside the scope of its mandatory powers. Principally, the FOS's legal basis comes from the Financial Services and Markets Act 2000 ('FSMA'). That legislation updated the existing law of financial regulation (which largely came from the Financial Services Act 1986). It created the Financial Services Authority ('FSA') to oversee regulation (now known, since 2012, as the Financial Conduct Authority ('FCA')). The 2000 Act also created the FOS, bringing together a wide array of existing ombudsman (including the Insurance Ombudsman and Banking Ombudsman). Until 1 December 2001, the FOS applied the rules of the scheme under which the complaint would previously have been brought. Since that date, it has applied the provisions in DISP, to which we shall now turn.

The FCA Handbook: DISP

The FOS's rules and procedures are principally set out in the FCA Handbook. Specifically, they are contained in the chapter called 'Dispute Resolution: Complaints' (or 'DISP', as it is known).

The FCA Handbook is made under the FCA's powers pursuant to the Financial Services and Markets Act. It is a form of secondary legislation. It is divided into a series of sections. Its scope is wide, covering everything to identifying who falls within the scope of regulation, to the standards and duties with which they must comply, and what happens when things go wrong. This last issue is where the FOS comes in.

DISP is that part of the Handbook that deals with complaints brought against respondents before the FOS.[2] It contains both 'Rules' and 'Guidance'. The former are denoted by the presence of an 'R' after the relevant provision (e.g. 1.1.1R). The latter are denoted with a 'G'. In general terms, rules create binding obligations on those who provide financial services in the UK, often referred to below as 'firms'. But guidance is not binding in the same way. Instead, it sets out explana-

2 See the Introduction to DISP.

tions, information as to what may be needed in order to ensure compliance, and recommended (but not mandatory) conduct.

The FCA Handbook: Glossary

Many words within the FCA Handbook are defined terms: all such defined terms are italicised in the text and, when viewed online, can be clicked to show the definition. When considering FCA Rules and Guidance it is important to consider such definitions.

How the FOS is set up

The FOS is a corporate body (in fact a limited company) known as the Financial Ombudsman Service Limited. It is the 'scheme operator' required by s.225 of FSMA to oversee and run the ombudsman service.

At the head of the FOS is a chairman and the board, whose members are directors of the FOS. Each are appointed and liable to be removed from office by the FCA.[3] The complaints themselves are determined by a series of ombudsmen and adjudicators. FSMA makes provision for a Chief Ombudsman,[4] who is responsible for leading the panel of ombudsmen. Both the FOS and the Chief Ombudsman are required to submit a report each year to the FCA on the discharge of their functions.[5] The FOS is also required to produce annual budgets and plans.[6]

Each of the documents that the FOS is required to produce can be found on its website.

---

3 FSMA, Schedule 17, Part II, paragraph 3.

4 FSMA, Schedule 17, Part II, paragraph 5.

5 Schedule 17, Part II, paragraph 7 of FSMA.

6 Schedule 17, Part II, paragraphs 9 and 9A of FSMA.

Sources of information

The FOS website[7] contains a whole host of information. Much is aimed at complainants, who are generally acting 'in person' (i.e. without lawyers). For those subject to the FOS's jurisdiction and those who advise them, more detailed information can be found in the FOS's 'online technical resource', which sets out guidance on a range of issues such as how the decision making process works to how the FOS calculates compensation. This guidance is obviously more detailed than that which can be found on the consumer-friendly parts of the FOS website.

The Ombudsman News is a regular publication from the FOS discussing contemporary issues facing the FOS. Each issue also includes case studies on a particular topic, giving guidance to how the FOS reached its decisions in particular complaints. Recent editions have looked at regular complaints arising out of travel insurance,[8] or accounts being used as 'money mule' accounts.[9]

When considering whether the FOS complied with the rule of law, the Court of Appeal in *R (Heather Moor & Edgecomb) v FOS* [2008] EWCA Civ 642 appeared somewhat concerned by the fact that decisions were not (at that time) published by the FOS.[10]

However, since 1 April 2013, the FOS has published the final decisions of ombudsmen, on http://www.ombudsman-decisions.org.uk/. If one is looking to understand what the FOS is likely to think 'fair and reasonable' (the standard the FOS applies when determining a dispute) in particular circumstances, it is therefore possible to see the approach taken in previous cases. FOS decisions are not precedents, but if a party wants to argue for a particular result, it can be useful to show how very similar facts have been dealt with previously.

---

7 http://www.financial-ombudsman.org.uk

8 Issue 143, January 2018.

9 Issue 139, January 2017.

10 See [85].

There have also been occasions in the past when the FOS decided to publish anonymised provisional decisions, in areas where it was seeing multiple complaints. So, in October 2012 the FOS was starting to see an upswing in complaints relating to interest rate hedging products and it decided to issue two provisional decisions on typical facts, setting out its approach. Final decisions on the same facts were then published in July 2013 (still anonymised). This approach may have been necessary before the database of decisions was introduced, and is probably no longer such, but these publications were useful in telling the industry the FOS's view on typical and repeated fact patterns.

The FOS as the source of new law

There have been occasions on which the FOS's approach to determining complaints has not only differed from the law as applied by the courts (see Chapter 11), but where the law has subsequently followed the FOS's approach. In particular, there had been longstanding criticisms on English law's approach to minor non-disclosures when applying for insurance policies, and breaches of warranties within insurance policies. The FOS led the way in adopting a more flexible approach than that used in the courts, and that approach subsequently found its way into the Consumer Insurance (Disclosure and Representations) Act 2012 and the Insurance Act 2015.

Otherwise, FOS decisions do not give rise to binding precedents.

The relationship between the FOS and the FCA

The relationship between the FOS and the FCA is principally set out in Schedule 17, part II of FSMA.

Paragraphs 2 and 3A of that Schedule imposes a series of basic duties on the FCA. They include, amongst other things:

1. A duty to take such steps as are necessary to ensure the FOS is capable of exercising its functions.

2. Making rules defining the FOS's compulsory jurisdiction.

3. Making rules defining the FOS's voluntary jurisdiction.

4. Specifying the maximum amount which the FOS is able to award as compensation.

5. Approving rules made by the FOS determining how costs of complaints are to be allocated.

6. Appointing and removing members of the FOS's board.

The FCA is also required to exercise its various functions in a way which is consistent with ensuring the FOS constitutes an 'ADR entity' within the meaning of the EU's Directive 2013/11/EU on Consumer ADR.

Further detail as to the relationship between the FOS and FCA can be found in a memorandum of understanding entered into between them on 18 December 2015.[11] The purpose of that memorandum is to describe how the two bodies are to cooperate with each other in performing their functions under paragraphs 2 and 3A of Schedule 17 of FSMA. The memorandum was required to be executed pursuant to paragraph 3A(2) of that Schedule in FSMA.

In broad terms, the memorandum sets out that whilst it is the FCA's duty as regulator to ensure that its relevant markets function well, it is the FOS's duty to operate a scheme under which disputes can be heard. According to the memorandum, the purpose of the FOS is to enable disputes to be resolved quickly and with minimum formality.[12]

The memorandum also sets out the way in which the FOS's governance is to be handled.[13] This provides further guidance as to how the FCA is to exercise its functions over things such as reviewing the FOS's budgets and reports, and appointing the FOS's directors. Paragraph 14 of the

11 https://www.fca.org.uk/publication/mou/mou-fos.pdf.

12 See paragraph 6.

13 Paragraphs 11 – 13.

memorandum provides details of how the FOS and FCA are to cooperate so as to ensure that their approaches are '*complementary and consistent*'. There is also an agreement for the FOS and FCA to disclose information with one another for the purposes of them helping to discharge their functions.[14]

14 Paragraphs 18 and 19.

CHAPTER TWO
THE COMPLAINT

Central to the role of the FOS is the idea that it is given responsibility for determining 'complaints'. The concept of a 'complaint' is one that appears throughout DISP, so it makes sense to consider this first, before going on to look at the FOS's jurisdiction (as to which, see the following chapters).

For most of DISP, 'complaints' are defined in the Glossary of the FCA Handbook as *'any oral or written expression of dissatisfaction'* about financial services, which:

- alleges that loss has been caused by an activity of a respondent, including financial loss, material distress or material convenience; and
- relates to an activity of that respondent, or of any other respondent with whom that respondent has some connection in marketing or providing financial services or products, which comes under the jurisdiction of the FOS.

This is obviously meant to be a very broad definition, and it is unlikely to cause too many difficulties in practise.

Given the informal nature of the FOS and the fact that most complainants will be unsophisticated in relation to the law and financial services, complaints are not like statements of case used in court proceedings. They can be very informal, and the FOS is not limited to the complaint as formulated by the complainant. Instead, it may reach a decision on a basis other than that put forward by the complainant.[1] Indeed, it is part of the FOS's job to determine the nature of the complaint.[2]

---

1 *R (Green) v FOS* [2003] EWHC 338 (Admin) at [41].

2 *R (Full Circle Asset Management Ltd) v FOS* [2017] EWHC 323 (Admin) at [53].

The FOS website explains that a complainant should '*tell us if you're unhappy*'[3] with the conduct of a respondent and allows complaints to be pursued by phone,[4] online, or by the completion of a complaint form.

In *R (Calland) v FOS* [2013] EWHC 1327 (Admin), the court accepted that the FOS was right to consider complaints, even though the 'expression of dissatisfaction' was made to the FCA (then FSA), which then took an active role in referring complaints to the FOS. The FOS then contacted the individuals and the individuals asked that the complaint be dealt with. It was suggested that the FSA or the FOS had solicited the complaints.[5] The court referred to this as a 'somewhat tangled way' for the complaint to arise, but had no doubt that the FOS was entitled to consider it.[6]

It is not necessary for the complainant to pursue the complaint his/herself if they authorise somebody else to do so.[7]

3 http://www.financial-ombudsman.org.uk/consumer/complaints.htm

4 As occurred in *R (Bankole) v FOS* [2012] EWHC 3555 (Admin). See [6].

5 See [21] and [55].

6 At [57] and [120].

7 DISP 2.7.2R.

CHAPTER THREE
THE FOS'S COMPULSORY AND VOLUNTARY JURISDICTIONS

The FOS is only able to hear those complaints which are within its jurisdiction. Whilst the FOS will take a view on whether it has jurisdiction, it will ultimately be for the courts to decide if the FOS got it right. It is a matter of statutory construction what the limits of the FOS's jurisdiction are, and if needs be they can be determined by way of judicial review (see Chapter 17).

Despite the number of jurisdictional hurdles which a complainant must overcome, it should in most cases be clear when the FOS has jurisdiction and when it does not.

The FOS will have jurisdiction where:[1]

1. The complaint falls within either its compulsory or voluntary jurisdiction, as dealt with in this chapter.

2. The complaint falls within the FOS's territorial jurisdiction - see Chapter 4.

3. The complainant is eligible – see Chapter 5.

4. The complaint has been brought in time – see Chapter 6.

The compulsory and voluntary jurisdictions place limits on both the types of activity in respect of which the FOS can hear complaints, and also who can be a respondent to a FOS complaint. We consider these issues below.

1 See DISP 2.2.1R.

The compulsory jurisdiction: respondents

As the name suggests, the compulsory jurisdiction sets out the mandatory jurisdiction of the FOS over some respondents and their activities.[2]

The FCA Handbook's Glossary provides a lengthy and broad definition of 'respondent'. For most complaints, it is sufficient to note that the definition includes 'firms' and payment service providers. As 'firm' is itself defined by reference to all authorised persons, it is normally sufficient to check whether the intended respondent can be found on the Financial Services Register.[3]

For more unusual situations, it will be necessary to consider the definitions in the FCA Handbook carefully. Some such situations include the following:

1. Certain people who formerly carried out roles that would have made them subject to the FOS's jurisdiction are covered. An example is a person who used to be an authorised firm but is no longer such at a time when the complaint is made. To avoid the complaint slipping through the cracks, the FOS will have jurisdiction over such a respondent, provided that at the time the act or omission giving rise to a complaint occurred, the compulsory jurisdiction rules covered the activity in question.[4]

2. Complaints can also be pursued against entities that have assumed liabilities for a predecessor.[5]

3. Many IFAs are not themselves authorised, and act via a 'network' which is authorised under FSMA.[6] In this situation,

2 FSMA, s.226.

3 https://register.fca.org.uk/

4 Glossary definition of 'respondent'; and FSMA, s. 226(2)(c).

5 FSMA, s. 234B.

6 Under FSMA, s. 39.

the IFA acts as an 'appointed representative' of the network, and FOS complaints can be pursued against the network.[7]

4. Activities covered by FSMA may be provided by people such as solicitors and accountants, who are regulated by their own professional bodies. In general, these are 'professional firms' and are not within the definition of a 'firm' in the FCA Handbook unless separately authorised by the FCA (an 'authorised professional firm'). There is a further complication here: DISP 2.3.4R states that the FOS will not consider complaints about authorised professional firms if the complaint relates solely to 'non-mainstream regulated activities' which can be handled by the firm's professional body.

The compulsory jurisdiction: activities

FSMA, s. 226(4) provides that only 'regulated activities', or activities which could be made regulated activities, can be subject to the FOS's compulsory jurisdiction.[8]

Often there will be no dispute about the relevant activities. Most 'financial services' as usually described are covered, particularly those provided to retail customers. Accordingly, almost anything done by a bank, an insurance company or similar institution will be capable of being considered by the FOS. Matters become more complicated away from that central scenario, and have led to the FOS and the courts grappling with questions such as whether tax advice also constitutes financial advice.[9]

---

7 DISP 2.3.3G.

8 Regulated activities are defined by FSMA, s.22 and set out in the Financial Services and Markets Act 2000 (Regulated Activities) Order 2001, more commonly referred to as 'the RAO'.

9 *R (Chancery (UK) LLP) v FOS* [2015] EWHC 407 (Admin).

A list of activities covered by the compulsory jurisdiction is set out in DISP 2.3.1R, and covers firms carrying on one or more of the following:

1. **Regulated activities other than auction regulation bidding.** A consideration of what constitutes a 'regulated activity' is outside the scope of this book. For the most part, the reader will be able to find a list in the Glossary of the FCA Handbook.[10] The more important will include: (i) accepting deposits; (ii) effecting / carrying out contracts of insurance; (iii) dealing in investments as agent or principal, or arranging deals in investments; and (iv) arranging regulated mortgage contracts.

2. **Payment services.** This covers those activities caught by the Payment Services Regulations.[11] Many day-to-day retail banking activities associated with operating current accounts will be caught, as will money remittance services.[12]

3. **Consumer buy-to-let ('CBTL') business.** In other words, acting as a buy to let lender, arranger or adviser, as each of those terms are defined in the Glossary to the FCA Handbook.

4. **Lending money secured by a charge on land.**

5. **Lending money.**[13] However this does not cover providing 'restricted credit' insofar as this is not a 'credit-related regulated

10 Full consideration of 'regulated activities' will also need to focus on the provisions of the RAO.

11 The relevant regulations depend on the date of the activity in question: if it occurred on before 13 January 2018 the Payment Services Regulations 2009 are applicable. After that date, see the Payment Services Regulations 2017.

12 A list is provided in reg. 2(1) and Schedule 1 of the relevant regulations.

13 It is an open question whether the mere lending of money is a regulated activity. The FCA do not consider that loans are '*instruments acknowledging or creating indebtedness*' within art. 77 of the RAO: see the FCA's letter to LMA dated 17 July 2014, responding to the Court of Appeal's decision in *Fons v Corporal Ltd* [2014] EWCA Civ 304 (where it was held in the context of the contracts being considered there that a 'debenture' could include a loan). Of course, it is the Court, not the FCA, which finally determines the scope of the RAO.

activity'.[14] By way of explanation, 'restricted credit' refers to loans from a firm to a consumer which can only be used to pay a supplier as a result of an existing arrangement between a supplier and a firm. A common example might include financing arrangements between car dealers and finance companies. The definition of 'restricted credit' does not include loans secured by charges over land or payments by plastic cards (as long as they are not store cards).

6. **Paying money by a plastic card which is not a store card where this is not a credit-related regulated activity.**

7. **Providing ancillary banking services**, including things such as operating cash machines, foreign currency exchanges, safe deposit boxes and account aggregation services.[15]

8. **Giving non-personal recommendation advice**. This covers the regulated activity specified in art.53(1) of the RAO and which does not amount to a personal recommendation.

Activities that are 'ancillary' to all of these activities are also caught. In particular, DISP 2.3.1R states that advice in connection with any of the activities above is ancillary to it.

The FOS is also able to consider a complaint under the compulsory jurisdiction if it relates to an act or omission by:

1. An investment firm[16] authorised under MiFID when providing investment services[17] or ancillary services by an investment firm

---

14 A list of 'credit-related regulated activities' can be found in Parts II and IIIA of the RAO (especially arts. 26A, 36H, 39D, 39E, 39F, 39G, 53DA, 60B, 60N, 89A and 89B).

15 DISP 2.1.5G.

16 An investment firm being defined for most purposes as a person whose regular occupation or business is the provision of one or more investment services to third parties and / or the performance of one or more investment activities on a professional basis.

2. A CRD credit institution when providing one or more investment services.

3. An investment firm authorised under MiFID or a CRD credit institution when selling structured deposits (i.e. the activity in art. 3 of the RAO) to clients, or advising clients on them.

4. A collective portfolio management investment firm when providing the activities permitted by art. 6(3) of the Undertakings for Collective Investment in Transferable Securities Directive.

5. A collective portfolio management investment firm when providing the activities permitted by article 6(4) of the Alternative Investment Fund Management Directive.

The FOS can also consider complaints about acts carried out by MiFID investment firms that are preparatory to the provision of an investment or ancillary service and which is an integral part of such a service: see DISP 2.3.1BG.

DISP 2.1.4R defines carrying on activity as including: (i) '*offering, providing or failing to provide a service in relation to an activity*'; (ii) '*administering or failing to administer a service in relation to an activity*'; and (iii) '*the manner in which a respondent has administered its business, provided that the business is an activity subject to the [FOS] jurisdiction*'.

This is cast in very broad language, but is not unlimited. The service or conduct subject to a complaint must be '*in relation to*' an activity or related to the '*manner in which*' the respondent carries out business. Complaints about wholly ancillary activities that have nothing to do with how the respondent carries on its business will not be caught by the FOS's jurisdiction. The definition of activity also puts beyond

17 Defined in the Glossary as being, amongst other things, the reception and transmission of orders in relation to one or more financial instruments, execution of orders on behalf of clients, portfolio management, the making of a personal recommendation, and the operation of a multilateral trading facility or organised trading facility.

doubt that a failure to do something is caught just as much as a positive act is.

That introduction aside, we will now consider in more depth some of the main types of activity that are within the FOS's compulsory jurisdiction, and to whom this applies.

Activities by payment service providers and electronic money issuers

These are covered by DISP 2.3.2AR and 2.3.2BR. The purpose is to extend the FOS's jurisdiction over entities that are not firms but which are providing payment services, issuing electronic money, or carrying on credit-related regulated activities insofar as they are carried out by payment service providers or electronic money issuers. The types of activities caught by DISP 2.3.2AR and 2.3.2BR also includes activities that are ancillary to the foregoing. Such ancillary activities include advice about these matters.

A payment service provider is defined in the Glossary to the FCA Handbook as including for the purposes of DISP: (i) authorised or small payment institutions (i.e. those institutions that are included in the Financial Services Register); (ii) EEA Authorised Payment Institutions (i.e. a person authorised in an EEA state other than the UK to provide payment services under the Payment Services Director. Provision is also made for firms based in Gibraltar); (iii) Post Office Ltd; and (iv) the Bank of England and Central European Bank.

The definition of electronic money issuer follows a similar format, including amongst others authorised and small electronic money institutions, as well as their EEA authorised counterparts.

Activities by CBTL firms

DISP 2.3.2BAR provides that the FOS has jurisdiction over complaints relating to acts and omissions by CBTL firms carrying on CBTL (i.e. consumer buy-to-let) business.

Activities by designated credit reference agencies and designated finance platforms

By DISP 2.3.2DR, the FOS can consider complaints under the compulsory jurisdiction if related to acts or omissions by designated credit reference agencies and finance platforms in carrying on either (i) the activity of providing credit information;[18] or (ii) ancillary activities thereto (including advice).

A 'designated credit reference agency' is one which is designated under Reg. 9 of the Small and Medium Sized Business Regulations 2015. These Regulations impose various obligations and duties on credit reference agencies to provide credit information about small and medium sized businesses.

Transitional provisions: Consumer Credit Jurisdiction

Prior to 1 April 2014, the FOS had a consumer credit jurisdiction. This was given to the FOS by virtue of s.226A of FSMA. It covered complaints in connection with consumer credit activities by respondents who were authorised under s.34A of the Consumer Credit Act 1974.

The consumer credit jurisdiction was (prior to 1 April 2014) set out in DISP 2.4.1R. The FOS had jurisdiction under its consumer credit jurisdiction if: (i) it was not covered by the compulsory jurisdiction; and (ii) it related to an act or omission by a licensee in carrying on either consumer credit activities or ancillary activities thereto.

'Consumer credit activities' were defined in the Glossary as meaning, amongst other things: (i) providing credit / being a creditor under a regulated consumer credit agreement; (ii) the bailment of goods under a regulated consumer hire agreement; and (iii) certain credit brokerage activities.

---

18 Small and Medium Sized Business (Credit Information) Regulations 2015

However, that jurisdiction no longer has a separate existence. To prevent complainants from finding themselves without a right of recourse, transitional provisions were implemented.[19]

A complaint made under the FOS's consumer credit jurisdiction before 1 April 2014 is to continue under s.226 of FSMA (the compulsory jurisdiction).

A complaint made on or after 1 April 2014 but which relates to an act or omission before that date will be dealt with under the s.226 jurisdiction if: (i) it could have been dealt with under s.226A (disregarding whether the complainant would have been eligible under the rules made for the purposes of the consumer credit jurisdiction and whether the complaint would have fallen within a description specified in those rules); (ii) the complainant is eligible; and (iii) the complainant wishes to have their complaint dealt with under the scheme.

Transitional provisions: Activities by firms and unauthorised persons subject to a former scheme

The FOS has jurisdiction over certain complaints that previously belonged (pre-2001) to the FOS's predecessors and also the General Insurance Council and Mortgage Code Arbitration Scheme (prior to 2005 and 2004 respectively). Transitional arrangements exist for these former schemes, but they are now of largely historical interest. If relevant, see DISP 2.3.2G.

Consumer redress schemes

One of the FCA's more important regulatory tools can be found in FSMA, s. 404. This gives it the power to set up consumer redress schemes if amongst other things it appears to the FCA that '*there may have been a widespread or regular failure by relevant firms to comply with requirements applicable to the carrying on by them of any activity*'.

---

19 DISP 2.3.2-AG and the Financial Services and Markets Act 2000 (Regulated Activities) (Amendment) (No.2) Order 2013, Art 11.

Obviously, it is necessary to ensure that the consumers who have a right to redress pursuant to a s. 404 scheme are adequately protected when determinations under them are made. To that end, DISP 2.3.2CR provides that a complainant who (i) is not satisfied with a redress determination made by a respondent under a consumer redress scheme; or (ii) considers that a respondent has failed to make a redress determination in accordance with a consumer redress scheme can be heard by the FOS.[20]

The FOS has jurisdiction to consider such complaints as follows:

1. A complaint can only be referred under DISP 2.3.2CR if made by a 'complainant'.

2. The term 'consumer redress scheme' is defined for the purposes of the Handbook as one imposed under FSMA s. 404 on authorised persons, payment service providers or electronic money issuers. It also includes those imposed on a particular firm, payment service provider or electronic money issuer by a requirement of its authorisation. This is a slightly different definition from that used in s.404.

3. The FOS's jurisdiction under these provisions relates to 'redress determinations'. This is tightly defined as a written communication from a respondent under a consumer redress scheme which: (i) sets out the results of the respondent's determination under the scheme; (ii) encloses a copy of the FOS's standard explanatory leaflet; and (iii) informs the complainant that if he is dissatisfied, he may make a complaint to the FOS and must do so within 6 months.

If a complaint is to be made about a redress scheme, the requirements of DISP 2.3.2CR must be fulfilled. This can be seen from *R (Mazarona Properties Ltd) v FOS* [2017] EWHC 1135 (Admin), which related to a bank's review of interest rate hedging products under an agreement with the FCA. As this was not a consumer redress scheme under FSMA,

---

20 The compulsory jurisdiction is extended by FSMA, s. 404B(11).

s. 404, the FOS did not have jurisdiction under the provisions discussed above.

Section 404B of FSMA also makes provision for how awards should be made under this head of jurisdiction. In particular, s. 404B(4) grants the FOS the power to decide what the determination under the redress scheme ought to have been. This can include ordering a money payment, in which case the order must not exceed the FOS's usual monetary limit (see Chapter 13). The FOS also has the power to order that respondents take specific actions (s.404B (8)).

The Voluntary Jurisdiction

Even if the FOS does not have jurisdiction under the compulsory scheme, it may have jurisdiction under the voluntary scheme.

The statutory basis for this can be found in s.227 of FSMA, which sets out the requirements for a complaint to be heard under the scheme. They are that:

1. The complainant is eligible and wishes to have the complaint dealt with under the scheme.

2. At the time the act or omission is said to have occurred, the respondent was participating in the scheme.

3. At the time the complaint is referred under the scheme, the respondent has not withdrawn from the scheme in accordance with its provisions.

4. The act or omission to which the complaint relates occurred when the voluntary jurisdiction rules were in force in relation to the activity in question.

5. The complaint cannot be dealt with under the compulsory jurisdiction.

These requirements are elaborated on in DISP 2.5.1R. In order for a complaint to be brought under the voluntary jurisdiction, it must be in respect of what DISP calls a 'VJ participant'. These are entities which have signed up to the FOS's jurisdiction by contractual agreement. They include certain banks, insurance companies, investment companies, mortgage and insurance intermediaries, amongst others.[21]

DISP 2.5.1R also sets out certain restrictions on the types of activity to which the voluntary jurisdiction applies. It must not be covered by the compulsory jurisdiction and it must be one of the following:

1. An activity carried on after 28 April 1988 that was not regulated at the time of the act or omission complained of, but was so regulated when the VJ participant joined the scheme (or became an authorised person, whichever is the later). As explained in DISP 2.5.3G, the purpose of this provision is to ensure that activities that would be covered by the compulsory jurisdiction but which are not covered by the transitional provisions in DISP 2.3.2R are caught.

2. A financial services activity (which term is undefined) carried on after commencement of s.19 FSMA (1 December 2001) by a VJ participant which was covered in respect of that activity by a former scheme immediately before the commencement of s.19 FSMA.

3. Activities which as at 3 January 2018 would be covered by the compulsory jurisdiction if carried out from a UK establishment. A list of these activities (of which there are many) can be found in DISP 2, Annex 1G.

4. Lending money secured by a charge on land.

5. Lending money other than restricted credit where that is not a credit-related regulated activity.

21 For further details of the businesses caught, see: http://www.financial-ombudsman.org.uk/faq/businesses/vj.html.

6. Paying money by a plastic card (excluding a store card where that is not a credit-related regulated activity).

7. Providing ancillary banking services.

8. Acting as an intermediary for a loan secured by a charge over land.

9. Acting as an intermediary for general insurance business or long-term insurance business.

10. National Savings and Investments' business.

Or in any case ancillary activities (including advice) carried on by the VJ participant in connection with the above.

DISP 2.5.5R also provides that the voluntary jurisdiction covers acts or omissions that occurred before the VJ participant was participating in the voluntary jurisdiction and also irrespective of whether the act or omission occurred before or after commencement (i.e. 1 December 2001), either if the complaint could have been dealt with under a former scheme or it has been agreed in the standard terms pursuant to which the VJ participants partake in the voluntary jurisdiction.[22]

As can be seen, the scope of the voluntary jurisdiction is broad. There may be some overlap with the compulsory jurisdiction,[23] in which case that jurisdiction takes precedence.

22 The terms are made under FSMA, Schedule 17, paragraph 18.

23 DISP 2.5.2G.

CHAPTER FOUR
THE FOS'S TERRITORIAL JURISDICTION

In this chapter, we consider the FOS's territorial jurisdiction. As set out below, the essence of the FOS's jurisdiction is that it will only apply if the activities in question were carried out from a UK establishment.

It is necessary, however, to distinguish between the compulsory and voluntary jurisdictions.

Compulsory jurisdiction

The relevant provisions here are DISP 2.6.1R and 2.6.2G.

The FOS will not have jurisdiction unless the activities in question are carried out from a UK establishment.

In the case of firms, it is enough for the appointed representatives under s.39 of FSMA to carry on business from such an establishment. In the case of payment service providers or electronic money issuers, it is enough that their agencies carry on business from such an establishment.

The jurisdiction also covers incoming EEA firms, incoming EEA authorised payment institutions, incoming EEA authorised electronic money institutions and incoming Treaty Firms. There must be a UK establishment; complaints about services provided from outside the UK are not covered other than EEA Undertakings for Collective Investment in Transferable Securities ('UCITS') management companies and Alternative Investment Funds Managers ('AIFM') management functions if they are carried out from an establishment in another EEA state pursuant to their rights to provide cross-border services.[1]

1 DISP 2.6.2G and DISP 2.6.1R (2).

So the key requirement is the need for an establishment in the UK. The concept of an 'establishment' is one which derives from EU law.

Article 49 of the Treaty on the Functioning of the European Union recognises two different types of establishment, the first being the setting up and management of (for instance) companies, firms or other undertakings. The second, which is likely to be the contentious issue insofar as the FOS's jurisdiction is concerned, is the setting up of agencies, branches and subsidiaries, irrespective of whether these have separate legal personality. The Court of Justice of the European Union has said that an establishment requires both a permanent presence in the host state and also the carrying on of genuine economic activities.[2]

Moreover, in order for the FOS to have jurisdiction the business in question must be carried on from the establishment. It is not enough that a respondent has a UK establishment if the complaint relates to business that was carried on from an establishment outside the UK.

Voluntary jurisdiction

This is even more restrictive. The VJ participant must either carry on the activities in question from an establishment in the UK or elsewhere in the EEA and additionally: (i) the activity must be directed wholly or partly at the UK; (ii) any contracts concerning the activity must be governed by English/Welsh, Scots or Northern Irish law;[3] and (iii) the VJ participant must have notified 'appropriate regulators' in its home state[4] that it intends to participate in the voluntary jurisdiction.[5]

2 See, for instance, *Case C-386/04 Centro di Musicologia Walter Stauffer* [2006] ECR I-8203.

3 The rules for determining the choice of law of a contract will be governed by the Rome I Regulation 593/2008.

4 What constitutes the home state changes depending on the type of firm or business in question. A detailed list is provided in the definition of 'home state' in the Handbook's Glossary. It is normally, but not always, the place of the registered or head office, but can include a place of residence (particularly where natural persons are concerned) or the place where business is carried on.

5 DISP 2.6.4R.

This last requirement has the potential to cause unfairness when the participant has not given the appropriate notice, and is therefore able to avoid the FOS's jurisdiction.

Does it make a difference if the complainant is outside the UK?

The answer here is a clear 'no': see DISP 2.6.5G. There is no requirement that a complainant lives or is based in the UK.

CHAPTER FIVE
WHO IS AN ELIGIBLE COMPLAINANT?

In order to bring a claim, the complainant must be eligible. The eligibility enquiry has two limbs to it.

The first is the 'who' requirement: is the complainant a type of person that can bring a complaint before the FOS?

The second is the 'relationship' requirement: is the complainant complaining about a relevant relationship?

The complainant

DISP 2.7.3R provides a list of eligible complainants. It must be a person[1] that is one of the following: (i) a consumer; (ii) a micro-enterprise; (iii) a small charity; (iv) a trustee of a small trust; or (iv) a CBTL customer.

We discuss each type of eligible complainant below.

<u>A consumer</u>

This means a person acting for the purposes which are wholly or mainly outside an individual's trade, business, craft or profession.[2]

In *R (Bluefin Insurance Services Ltd) v FOS* [2014] EWHC 3413 (Admin), Wilkie J considered this definition in the context of a director of a company who benefited from a Directors and Officers ('D&O') policy and who sought to complain to the FOS. It was held that he was not a consumer in view of the fact his company advanced his business interests and the policy covered his acts as a director. Thus, '*the subject*

---

1 Which includes for these purposes any natural or legal person, including a body corporate or unincorporated, and partnerships.

2 Glossary definition of 'consumer' as applicable to DISP.

matter of his complaint was wholly concerned with the potential loss arising from lack of insurance cover in respect of a liability which he had incurred in the course of his trade, business, or profession.'[3]

This conclusion rested on a different definition of consumer from that which now applies, but there is no reason to think that the current definition would have led to a different result.

It should be noted, however, that DISP refers not only to those acts wholly outside a person's trade, but covers also those which are '*mainly*' outside their business. This adds a degree of uncertainty into what is meant by a consumer, as it is clear that some connection with business interests may be permissible.

It is probable, however, that the connection can at most be small if a person is to be a consumer, with the business connection being ancillary and minimal. Of interest is the case of *Ashfaq v International Insurance Co. of Hannover PLC* [2017] EWCA Civ 357, in the different context of the Unfair Terms in Consumer Contracts Regulations 1999. The court also considered ICOBS 2.1.1G(2) and 8.1.2R, which define consumer as someone acting mainly for purposes unrelated to their trade or profession. It was held that there was no real prospect of a claimant who was using a property covered by insurance for the business of letting to students establishing that he was a consumer.

It is also of note that the definition of consumer refers to an 'individual'. This should exclude, for instance, companies and partnerships[4] from the definition of consumer.

In contentious cases it may also be necessary to turn to EU law when considering the definition of a consumer.[5] In *R (Bluefin Insurance Services) v FOS* [2014] EWHC 3413 (Admin), the court considered that

3 See paragraph [125].

4 For the difficulties relating to how regulatory rules can apply to partnerships, see *Thomas v Triodos* [2017] EWHC 314 (QB) at [58].

5 The definition is the same as that in the Alternative Dispute Resolution for Consumer Disputes (Competent Authorities and Information) Regulations 2015, reg.3, which implement EU Directive 2013/11/EU.

the answer was clear-cut, but suggested that EU authorities might be useful in borderline cases.[6]

Micro-enterprises[7]

A micro-enterprise is an enterprise which employs fewer than 10 persons and has a turnover or annual balance sheet that does not exceed €2 million.

An enterprise is defined as including any person engaged in economic activity whatever the legal form. This is evidently intended to be a broad definition. It will catch self-employed individuals, family businesses engaged in craft or other activities, and partnerships or associations regularly engaged in economic activities.[8]

The time at which it is assessed whether the requirements of being a micro-enterprise are fulfilled will depend on what the complaint is about. By DISP 2.7.3R(2), if the complaint relates wholly or partly to payments services, it must be at the time of the conclusion of the payment service contract or at the time the complainant refers the complaint to the respondent. Otherwise, it must be at the time the complaint is referred to the respondent.

DISP 2.7.4G states that when assessing whether an enterprise is a micro-enterprise, account should be taken of the enterprise's partners or linked enterprises.[9] So if a parent company of the complainant does not meet the definition of a micro-enterprise, the complainant will not do so either.

---

6 At [97].

7 Statistics relating to complaints considered by the FOS about micro-enterprises can be found at: http://www.financial-ombudsman.org.uk/publications/pdf/Micro-enterprise-complaints-Aug-2015.pdf.

8 By way of example, this would presumably cover an unincorporated association comprised of volunteers running (say) a museum, provided that at least some form of economic activity was carried on (perhaps the invariable café or gift shop, no matter how small).

9 As those terms are defined in Recommendation 2003/361/EC of the Commission of 6th May 2003.

The scope of the FOS's jurisdiction for small and medium enterprises may expand in the future. At the time of writing, the FCA was consulting on whether to expand the jurisdiction in this area.[10]

Small charities

A charity is an eligible complainant if it has an annual income of less than £1 million at the time the complaint is referred to the respondent.[11] No further definitions or guidance are provided.

Trustees of small trusts

A trustee of a trust will be an eligible complainant if the trust that has a net asset value of less than £1 million at the time the complainant refers the complaint to the respondent.[12]

CBTL consumers

In relation to a consumer buy-to-let credit agreement, eligible complainants are either: (i) persons acting for purposes that are outside their trade, business or profession,[13] or (ii) a borrower under a CBTL credit agreement.

Note that, here, we are concerned with a 'person' (which will include companies and other legal entities) rather than just 'individuals'. It is also noteworthy that, unlike with the definition of 'consumer', the fact that the person is acting for purposes that are in any way connected with their business will be fatal to the suggestion they are a CBTL consumer under the first limb of the test.

---

10 FCA CP 18/3, January 2018: 'Consultation on SME access to the Financial Ombudsman Service and Feedback to DP15/7: SMEs as Users of Financial Services'.

11 DISP 2.7.3R.

12 DISP 2.7.3R.

13 Again, note that, unlike with the definition of '*consumer*', the fact that the person is acting for purposes that are in any way connected with their business will be fatal to the suggestion they are a CBTL customer under the first limb of the test.

Applying the definitions

Factually, working out whether a complainant is within the various requirements above may be quite difficult.

Whilst many companies could be expected to keep good accounting records (making it easier to tell if they are a 'micro-enterprise' for instance), that will not always be so. Doubtless aware of these potential difficulties, DISP 2.7.4G warns respondent firms that if are in doubt they should treat a complainant as if they were eligible. The FOS will then later determine eligibility by reference to appropriate evidence, such as audited accounts or VAT returns.

If a respondent firm is going to take a point on eligibility, they would do well to do so as soon as possible and make that clear (for instance, explaining to the would-be complainant that they will deal with them on a basis that is without prejudice to their right to dispute eligibility).

It has been said the question of whether a complainant is eligible is one of 'objective fact' and 'hard-edged criteria'.[14] This means that, on a judicial review arising out of a determination whether a complainant is eligible, the court will be able to decide the question for itself.

The relationship requirement

Even if a complainant is eligible they must still fulfil the relationship requirements. These are set out in DISP 2.7.6R. Essentially, the complaint must arise '*from matters relevant to one or more of the following relationships with the respondent*'.

The relationships referred to are 18 in number. The most important are likely to be as follows:

1. A customer, payment service user or electronic money holder of the respondent.[15] Also covered are potential customers,

14 See *R (Bluefin Insurance Services Ltd) v FOS* [2014] EWHC 3414 (Admin).

15 DISP 2.7.6R (1).

payment service users or electronic money holders.[16] Of these three terms, 'customer' is in practice the most important. It is defined in the Glossary to the FCA Handbook in a number of different ways depending on the activity in question, though in most cases the answer will be clear.

2. A person for whose benefit a contract of insurance was or was intended to be taken out with or through the respondent.[17] This is not limited to just the person who was a party to the insurance contract. Many home, motor or travel insurance policies will be taken out for the benefit of family members by one member of the household. The expansive definition of eligible complainant avoids knotty issues about who strictly was a party to the contract. DISP 2.7.7G gives the further example of employees who have the benefit of a group permanent health policy taken out by an employer for their benefit.

3. A person who gave the respondent a guarantee or security for a mortgage, loan, an actual or prospective regulated credit agreement, or any linked transaction under the Consumer Credit Act 1974.[18]

4. A person about whom information relevant to his financial standing is or was held by the respondent in providing credit references or credit information.[19] 'Providing credit references' concerns the furnishing of persons with information relevant to the financial standing of individuals or relevant recipients of credit, provided the information has been collected for that purpose.[20] 'Credit information' is defined to cover various items of information about sterling loans, sterling credit card accounts, sterling current accounts, as well as certain ancillary

16 DISP 2.7.6R (2).

17 DISP 2.6.7R (5).

18 DISP 2.7.6R (10).

19 DISP 2.7.6R (11) and (11A).

20 This phrase has the same meaning as the activity specified in art.89B of the RAO.

information.[21] DISP 2.7.6R(11B) also adds to the list of eligible complainants a person about whom 'specified information'[22] in relation to a 'finance application' was provided.[23]

5. A person from whom the respondent has sought to recover payment under a credit agreement or consumer hire agreement, irrespective of whether the respondent is a party to the agreement.[24] A complainant is also covered where the respondent has sought to exercise or enforce rights on behalf of a creditor or owner under a credit agreement or consumer hire agreement in carrying on debt administration.[25]

Miscellaneous eligible complainants

Even if the complainant does not strictly satisfy the eligibility requirements, they may be able to rely on DISP 2.7.2R. This is a narrow rule which provides that a complaint may be brought on behalf of an eligible complainant or a deceased person that would have been eligible. The person bringing the complaint must, however, be authorised by someone who would be an eligible complainant or be authorised 'by law'. The term 'by law' has presumably been added to cover, for instance, the executor of an estate. In these circumstances, the person so authorised need not themselves be an eligible complainant.

---

21 Small and Medium Sized Business (Credit Information) Regulations 2015, in particular reg. 2 and Schedule 1.

22 As that term is defined in reg.2 and Schedule 1 of the Small and Medium Sized Business (Finance Platforms) Regulations 2015/1946. Essentially, it covers the name of the business, its address, email address, phone number, the amount of finance requested, the type of finance, its legal structure, the duration of its trading, and the date by which it requires or has requested finance.

23 As that term is also defined in reg. 2 of the Small and Medium Sized Business (Finance Platforms) Regulations 2015/1946. Essentially, a request in any form for a finance facility.

24 DISP 2.7.6R (12)(a).

25 Debt administration is a regulated activity defined by art.39G of the RAO.

There is also a narrow exception to the eligibility rules under the FOS's transitional provisions: where a complainant who wishes to bring a complaint is not otherwise eligible, but could have brought a complaint under one of the former schemes that the FOS assumed responsibility for, they may be treated by the FOS as if they were eligible.[26] This is now of largely historical interest.

Exceptions

Even if a complainant would otherwise be eligible, it is still necessary to check whether they fall within one of the eligibility exceptions contained in DISP 2.7.9R and 2.7.10G. These exceptions are designed to ensure that large and sophisticated institutions, and those that are themselves authorised by the FCA, cannot complain to the FOS.

First, entities that are themselves firms, payment service providers, electronic money issuers, CBTL firms, designated credit reference agencies, designated finance platforms, or VJ participants who wish to bring a complaint in respect of activities which they are authorised to carry on are excluded.[27]

Secondly, in connection with the compulsory jurisdiction, a complainant will be ineligible if they are either a <u>professional client</u> or <u>eligible counterparty</u> in relation to the firm and activity in question at the time of the act or omission subject to the complaint.[28]

The terms 'professional client' or 'eligible counterparty' are references to the classification rules contained in COBS 3.5 and 3.6. A client will normally either be a retail client, professional client or eligible counterparty. The purpose of these rules is to change the degree of regulation by reference to how sophisticated the customer is.

26 DISP 2.7.8G, arising out of the Financial Services and Markets Act 2000 (Transitional Provisions) (Ombudsman Scheme and Complaints Scheme) Order 2001 or the Financial Services and Markets Act 2000 (Transitional Provisions) (Complaints Relating to General Insurance and Mortgages) Order 2004.

27 DISP 2.7.9R (1).

28 Except if they are a trustee of a pension scheme trust: DISP 2.7.9R (2).

A professional client will be a client that is either a *per se* professional client or an elective professional client.

Per se professional clients include authorised firms, insurance companies and other financial institutions. They also include 'large undertakings' meeting two of the following requirements: (i) a balance sheet total of €20 million; (ii) net turnover of €40 million; or (iii) ownership funds of at least €2 million. Bodies corporate that have share capital or net assets of at least £5 million are also caught. There are many more besides.[29]

Elective professional clients are clients that firms may treat as professional clients, provided that they meet the criteria set out in COBS 3.5.3R. Those criteria are that: (i) the firm must assess their expertise with the result that this gives them reasonable assurance that the client can make their own investment decisions; (ii) in connection with MiFID or equivalent third country business, the client meets one of the six additional requirements set out in COBS 3.5.3R; and (iii) the procedure for agreeing with the client that they are to be treated as a professional client has been complied with.

Eligible counterparties are defined in COBS 3.6. They again come in two types: *per se* eligible counterparties and elective eligible counterparties. They will typically be larger institutions.

29 They are listed in COBS 2.5.2R.

CHAPTER SIX
TIME LIMITS FOR COMPLAINTS TO THE FOS

There are tight time limits for referring a complaint to the FOS. It is clear from the rules that the FOS is responsible for considering whether a dispute has been referred in time, and its decision will only be capable of review on the usual grounds for judicial review (see Chapter 17).

First, a FOS complaint should not be brought too early. The FOS is intended to operate as a fall back if the firm has failed to resolve the complaint satisfactorily using its own complaint handling mechanisms.

Secondly, a FOS complaint can be dismissed if it is brought too late. There are two different events by reference to which it can be decided if the complainant is out of time. They are:

1. The final response issued by the relevant respondent (though we as we will see there is an exception for consumer redress schemes); or
2. The date of events in respect of which a complaint is made occurred.

The respondent's final response

The FOS's procedures are supposed to act as an alternative to the respondent's own complaint handling procedures, which the respondent is required to have in place by DISP 1.

DISP 1 draws a distinction between MiFID complaints[1] (which are dealt with in DISP 1.1A) and other complaints. Provided that the rule in DISP 1.1A is marked with an 'EU'[2], as opposed to the usual 'R' or

1 A MiFID complain is one which falls within the scope of EU Commission Delegated Regulation 2017/565, art. 26 and DISP 1.1A.3R.

2 Or is DISP 1.1A.39R which will also apply.

'G', it will apply to complaints from all clients (as that term is defined in MiFID) who are not otherwise eligible complainants, and thus will include retail clients, professional clients and eligible counterparties. Otherwise, all the provisions of DISP 1.1A (i.e. both those that are marked with an 'EU', 'R' and 'G') will apply provided that the complainant is eligible (even if they are also a retail client, professional client or eligible counterparty): see DISP 1.1A.6R. These rules do not impact on the question of whether a complaint can be brought before the FOS, which is governed by different parts of DISP.

DISP 1 requires the respondent to investigate complaints '*competently, diligently and impartially*' and to offer redress where it decides that it is appropriate.[3] As part of those procedures, the respondent is required to issue either a 'summary resolution communication'[4] or a 'final response'.[5] In practice, most complaints lead to a final response, and so for the remainder of this chapter we only refer to final responses.

In cases other than those relating to electronic money and payment services (so-called EMD or PSD complaints),[6] the final response should be issued by the respondent within 8 weeks of receipt of the complaint, and is a written response which sets out the respondent's position on the complaint. The respondent is required to enclose the FOS's explanatory leaflet and tell the complainant that, if they are dissatisfied with the resolution or response, they may be able to refer the complaint to the FOS. It should also include the FOS's website address. The respondent should also inform the complainant whether it (the respondent) will waive the time limits that apply to FOS claims (as discussed below) and, if not, it should refer explicitly to the time limits and the need to refer the complaint within them.[7]

---

3 DISP 1.4.1R and DISP 1.1A.20R.

4 DISP 1.5.4R.

5 DISP 1.6.2R.

6 As to which, see DISP 1.6.2A, requiring a final response within 15 business days or, exceptionally, 35 business days but only if a holding response has been sent within 15 business days.

7 DISP 1.6.2R.

If the respondent is unable to provide its final response within 8 weeks, then the respondent should set this out in a written response, but should also inform the complainant that they may now refer their complaint to the FOS.[8]

DISP 2.8.1R states that, unless the respondent consents, complainants may not refer their complaints to the FOS before either the final response has been provided or eight weeks have elapsed since the complainant complained and no final response has been forthcoming.[9]

Time limit from the final response

The final response is important in that it triggers the first of the time limits identified above: subject to the exceptions set out below, the FOS has no power to consider a complaint if it is referred to the FOS more than 6 months after the final response.[10]

DISP 2.8.3G refers to the need for a final response to refer to the six month time limit. The implication is that a final response which fails to do so will not start time running.

Subsequent correspondence after the final response does not extend time, absent a formal and clear withdrawal of the final response.[11]

Consumer redress schemes

If the complaint was considered under a consumer redress scheme, then there will be a 'redress determination' rather than a final response. Such a complaint may only be referred after the redress determination has been issued, or should have been issued under the time limits specified

8 DISP 1.6.2R(2).

9 Except for electronic money and payment services complaints, in which case the complaint can be referred after 15 business days if there has been no holding response, and after 35 business if there has been a holding response.

10 DISP 2.8.2R (1).

11 *R (Bankole) v FOS* [2012] EWHC 3555 (Admin) at [24].

by the scheme. The FOS has no jurisdiction to consider complaints raised more than six months after the redress determination.[12]

Time limit from the events in respect of which a complaint is made

The FOS also has no power to consider a complaint, if it is referred to the FOS after the later of:

1. Six years after the event complained of; or
2. Three years from the date on which the complainant became aware or ought reasonably to have become aware that they had cause for complaint.[13]

These time limits apply unless, in either case, a complaint was made to the respondent or the FOS within the relevant period and there is written acknowledgment or record of the complaint having been received. This wording is important: it means that complaints can be referred to the FOS outside of the time limits, as long as the complaint was referred to the respondent in time. In essence, the complaint to the respondent will stop time running, though the complainant will still need to refer their complaint within six months of receiving a final response from the respondent.

Again, this is subject to the exceptions set out below.

It should be noted that there is no equivalent of the fifteen year 'long-stop' date in the Limitation Act 1980.[14] In *R (Bamber) v FOS* [2009] EWCA Civ 593 the court rejected an argument that this was unlawful as abrogating the respondent's accrued rights under the 1980 Act. Accordingly, it seems clear that the FOS is not bound to apply its rules so as to ensure consistency with the law on limitation.

---

12 DISP 2.8.2R (1).

13 DISP 2.8.2R (2).

14 S. 15B of that Act, in relation to negligence claims not involving personal injuries.

Exception: the respondent consents

None of the time limits identified above apply where the respondent consents to the FOS considering the complaint, except in relation to complaints under consumer redress schemes.[15] Once a respondent has consented, it cannot withdraw that consent.[16]

Exception: exceptional circumstances

The time limits do not apply if there has been a failure to comply because of 'exceptional circumstances'.[17] DISP 2.8.4G gives the example of a complainant having been incapacitated.

Technical notes on the FOS's website provide further guidance on this exception,[18] which show that serious ill health may suffice, if the FOS is persuaded that the complainant delayed their complaint because of their treatment. If the respondent leads the complainant to think that the deadline is later than it really is, this may also provide exceptional circumstances. Other examples given are complainants on extended holidays, such that they do not see the final response, and complainants dealing with a family bereavement.

On the other hand, the FOS technical notes suggest that it will not extend time because complainants had previously believed that they had little prospect of success, or because of illnesses that did not prevent the complainant from corresponding with the respondent. Likewise, being busy at work or being made redundant are not thought of as 'exceptional'.

---

15 DISP 2.8.2R (5).

16 DISP 2.8.2AR.

17 DISP 2.8.2R (3).

18 http://www.financial-ombudsman.org.uk/publications/technical_notes/six-month-time-limit.htm#10

It seems that the FOS is not required to consider of its own motion whether this exception applies, at least if it is clear that they did not believe that to be the position on the facts before them. However, in some cases it would be sensible for the FOS specifically to address the issue to avoid unfairness or confusion and where that is so may have to raise the point itself.[19]

Exception: transitional arrangements

The usual time limits do not apply if the FOS is required under transitional arrangements to hear the complaint.[20]

Exception: pension transfers etc.

The six and three year time limits do not apply if the complaint concerns a contract or policy which is or was under review under the policies issued by the FSA in relation to Pension transfers and opt outs and FSAVC (i.e. a voluntary contribution arrangement in connection with certain types of occupational pension schemes) on 25 October 1994 and 28 February 2000 respectively.[21]

Likewise, provisions exist in relation to the sale of mortgage endowment policies to ensure that time for referring a complaint does not run until the complainant has been told that there is a high risk the policy will not produce a large enough sum to repay the mortgage at maturity.[22] Note that the requirement is for the complainant to be told there is a 'high risk'. Being told of the fact there was 'a risk' is not enough. Time will end three years after the relevant letter, provided that the complainant is told, at least six months before the final date to refer the

19 *R (Bankole) v FOS* [2012] EWHC 3555 (Admin) at [15] and [24].

20 DISP 2.8.2R and the FSMA 2000 (Transitional provisions) (Ombudsman Scheme and Complaints Scheme) Order 2001.

21 DISP 2.8.5R.

22 DISP 2.8.6G.

complainant, that the time to refer the complaint will expire at that date.[23]

The final exception relates to PPI complaints. Because of the widespread publicity about the sale of PPI, DISP 2.8.8G clarifies that mere knowledge that there was a problem with the sale of PPI 'generally' is not normally enough to start the three year time limit running to bring a complaint relating to a failure to disclose commission.[24]

The FOS has also imposed a long stop date on PPI claims. If the sale occurred before 29 August 2017 and the complaint expresses dissatisfaction about the sale, the complaint must be referred to the FOS before 29 August 2019 (provided there is written acknowledgement or some other record of the complaint having been received),[25] though this is not so if a failure to comply with that long stop date occurs due to exceptional circumstances.[26] Provision is also made for the respondent to consent to the complaint being heard out of time.[27]

---

23 DISP 2.8.7R (2). Time will instead run until a date specified in the explanation, which cannot be less than 6 months (DISP 2.8.7R (4).

24 See DISP App 3.3A.2E.

25 DISP 2.8.9R (2)(a).

26 DISP 2.8.2R (3).

27 DISP 2.8.9R (2)(c).

CHAPTER SEVEN
PROCEDURE: AN INTRODUCTION

This chapter and the following chapters look at the procedural steps of a FOS decision, from the FOS's receipt of an initial complaint from through to an ombudsman's final decision.[1]

In these chapters we do not address the tests that that the FOS will apply in order to resolve the complaint: those issues are discussed in Chapter 11. However, it is impossible to divorce the two issues entirely. The FOS is to determine complaints by reference to what is 'fair and reasonable', but that same test is relevant to the procedure adopted by the FOS, as we shall see below when considering the availability of oral hearings.

The starting point for the FOS's procedure is FSMA, s. 225(1): the FOS was set up so that '*certain disputes may be resolved quickly and with minimum formality by an independent person*'.

Consistent with this, the FOS is entitled to take a very different approach from a court of law.[2] In summary:

1. The FOS is inquisitorial rather than adversarial.
2. Oral hearings are the exception rather than the rule: the FOS will typically resolve a complaint based on written evidence and arguments.
3. The strict rules of evidence do not apply to the FOS.

Nevertheless, the FOS is a tribunal for the purpose of Article 6 of the European Convention on Human Rights,[3] and so its procedures should

1 There are circumstances in which the FOS will need to apply the rules of a former scheme: DISP 3.1.4G. Such former scheme rules are outside the ambit of this chapter.

2 Emphasised in *R (Heather Moor & Edgecomb) v FOS* [2009] EWHC 2701 (Admin) at [8].

3 *R (Calland) v FOS* [2013] EWHC 1327 (Admin) at [35].

comply with the requirements of that Article and should be concluded within a reasonable time.

The use of lawyers and claims management companies

Both complainants and respondents can use lawyers to represent them in relation to FOS complaints, and this is quite normal for larger disputes. However, the FOS takes the view that such assistance is not necessary, and that it prefers to hear from parties '*in their own words*'.[4] Given that costs are rarely awarded, the FOS also makes the point that the cost of lawyers for a complainant will generally have the effect of reducing any compensation they might get.

In some areas, it is also very common for complaints to be pursued by claims management companies on behalf of consumers. They are not prohibited, but the FOS generally discourages their use, stressing that the FOS is intended to be simple and accessible without assistance.[5]

In some areas, the vast majority of complaints are pursued by representatives: in 2016/2017, some 84.5% of PPI complaints were pursued by claims management companies on behalf of complainants.[6]

The role of adjudicators and ombudsmen

In this book, we regularly refer to the FOS as though it was the body making the decisions. This is used as short-hand, as FOS decisions are actually reached by ombudsmen, and a decision reached by an ombudsman is the final stage in resolving a complaint.

The DISP rules only talk about ombudsmen (not the FOS) and they also omit any reference to the adjudication stage of FOS complaints.

---

4 http://www.financial-ombudsman.org/publications/consumer-leaflet.htm

5 In relation to PPI claims:
http://www.financial-ombudsman.org/publications/ombudsman-news/94/94.pdf

6 FOS Annual Review 2016/2017, page 63.

In fact, many FOS complaints never reach ombudsmen and are dealt with by adjudicators (also referred to as case handlers). They undertake initial fact finding in relation to the complaint, and in a typical case they will produce their assessment of the complaint, complete with an assessment of the appropriate redress (if any). In essence, this is a preliminary decision, which either party can reject and escalate the complaint to an ombudsman for a final decision.

So, for example, an adjudicator may seek facts from both parties, before concluding that the complaint should lead to some form of compensation. If both parties accept that recommendation, then they will settle the complaint based on the adjudicator's view. If either party does not wish to accept the recommendation, the complaint will be referred to an ombudsman.

Although they do not feature in the rules, these assessments by adjudicators are the end-point for the vast majority of all FOS complaints. Only about 10% of complaints are resolved by ombudsmen.[7]

If a complaint is referred to an ombudsman, they will consider the adjudicator's investigations but are expected to form their own view of the facts, and may require further information from the parties, before issuing their decision (set out below). However, even once the matter has been referred to an ombudsman, the adjudicator will remain involved as the parties' main point of contact. Parties are not expected to communicate with the ombudsman directly.[8]

There is a large panel of ombudsmen, appointed as individuals of '*appropriate qualifications and experience*'.[9] There is no jurisdictional limit on an ombudsman considering any kind of complaint, but the

7 Annual review 2016/2017 showed that 38,619 complaints reached a final decision by an ombudsman, out of 336,381 resolved complaints. The numbers vary by year, but have consistently been around 10%.

8 http://www.financial-ombudsman.org.uk/publications/factsheets/what-happen-now-my-case-has-been-referred-to-an-ombudsman.pdf

9 FSMA, Schedule 17, Part II, para 4.

FOS states that typically ombudsman specialise in particular areas of complaint.[10]

A list of ombudsmen can be found on the FOS's website, which provides limited CVs for each of them.[11] A review of that list suggests that a great many of them are qualified solicitors or barristers, with some ombudsmen having risen through the FOS, from adjudicator to ombudsman. A few have come to the FOS from the financial services sector itself, but they appear to be in a minority.

From the panel of ombudsmen, a Chief Ombudsman is appointed.[12] The Chief Ombudsman has an important role in representing the FOS to the outside world, but has no special powers in relation to FOS complaints.

Timescales

Under the ADR Directive, complaints are supposed to be dealt with within 90 days save in 'highly complex disputes'.[13] The FOS's Annual Review for 2016/2017 stated that 83% of non-PPI complaints were dealt with within 3 months, though it should be noted that only about 10% of complaints are resolved by a final decision.[14] In our experience, few disputed complaints that go all the way to a final decision are resolved within 90 days.

---

10 FOS *a quick guide to… the role and work of our panel of ombudsmen*: http://www.financial-ombudsman.org.uk/publications/technical_notes/QG-ombudsman-panel.pdf

11 http://www.financial-ombudsman.org.uk/about/panel-ombudsmen.html

12 FSMA, Schedule 17, Part II, para 5.

13 Directive 2013/11/EU, Article 8(e).

14 Annual review 2016/2017 showed that 38,619 complaints reached a final decision by an ombudsman, out of 336,381 resolved complaints. The numbers vary by year, but have consistently been around 10%.

Despite the ADR Directive, the FOS does not have a set time limit in which it is required to resolve a complaint. There have been unusual examples of complaints that took 5 years to resolve.[15]

The length of time that the complaint actually takes will obviously depend upon the stage that it reaches: a complaint resolved by accepting an adjudicator's findings will generally be quicker than a complaint with a dispute about jurisdiction, followed by provisional and final decisions from an ombudsman.

The most recent data suggests that around two thirds of cases are resolved within three months, 80% of cases within six months, and 87% of cases within a year.

---

15 *R (Green) v FOS* [2012] EWHC 1253 (Admin)

CHAPTER EIGHT
DETERMINING JURISDICTION AND SUMMARY DISMISSAL OF COMPLAINTS

This chapter deals with three situations in which a complaint can be disposed of without a final decision on the merits, because:

1. The complaint is out of the FOS's jurisdiction.
2. The complaint is dismissed summarily for one of a number of reasons enumerated below.
3. The dispute is referred to another complaints scheme, or the court.

Determining jurisdiction

In the initial stages, the FOS will consider whether the complaint is within its jurisdiction. In most cases, this is likely to be a formality, and there will be no need for representations or a formal decision by an ombudsman.

In other cases, particularly where time limits appear to be in issue, it is likely that the FOS will want to investigate and the jurisdiction question can become a substantial stage of the FOS processes on its own.[1] The respondent can also require the FOS to reach a decision if it disputes jurisdiction on a complaint. When it does so, the FOS will then give both parties the chance to make representations.[2] Likewise, the FOS may take it upon itself to consider jurisdiction where it considers that the complaint might be outside of its jurisdiction.[3]

1 DISP 3.2.4R.

2 DISP 3.2.3R

3 DISP 3.2.4R.

In practice, in such cases, it will usually be an adjudicator who gathers evidence and expresses a view before the ombudsman produces a provisional decision and then a final decision on jurisdiction.

In one extreme example, a complaint was initiated in July 2005, and the respondent vigorously objected to jurisdiction. After delays that were largely due to the respondent itself, jurisdiction was not resolved until October 2009.[4]

If the FOS does not have jurisdiction, then the complaint will not proceed. A complainant unhappy with this conclusion would need to consider judicial review proceedings at this stage (see Chapter 17).

If the FOS concludes that it does have jurisdiction, then the complaint will continue. The FOS's stated position in court has been that it will continue to consider whether it has jurisdiction until the final decision on the merits.[5] A respondent that is unhappy with the outcome on jurisdiction appears therefore to have a choice whether to commence judicial review proceedings at this point, or after the final decision on the merits. For more detail on this question, see Chapter 17.

Dismissal of complaints without consideration

In addition to the possibility of a complaint being out of jurisdiction, DISP 3.3.4AR set out the current rules[6] for dismissing a complaint without consideration of the merits.

The current rules say that the FOS 'may' dismiss complaints on five grounds, which are set out below. Previously, the rules stated that the FOS 'must' consider whether to dismiss a case summarily. As the wording of the rules has changed, we consider that comments in cases

---

4 See *R (Calland) v FOS* [2013] EWHC 1327 (Admin) at [41-66].

5 *R (Chancery (UK) LLP) v FOS* [2015] EWHC 407 (Admin) at [78].

6 DISP 3.3.4R sets out the rules for complaints referred to the FOS before 9 July 2015. We assume that the FOS has already considered whether to dismiss such complaints.

suggesting an obligation on the FOS to consider dismissal probably no longer represent the law.[7]

If the FOS is considering dismissing a complaint on one of these grounds, then the complainant will be given an opportunity to make representations.[8]

The decision whether to dismiss a complaint summarily may be delegated to a designated member of staff.[9]

Although, typically, complaints are dismissed under these rules early on in the process, there is nothing to stop the FOS from dismissing complaints at any time.[10] It may be the case, for example, that evidence emerges late in the day to show that the complaint is frivolous or vexatious. Instead of proceeding to a final decision, the ombudsman could choose to dismiss the complaint.

Frivolous or vexatious complaints

The FOS may summarily dismiss a complaint if it considers that the complaint is 'frivolous or vexatious'.[11]

4,207 complaints were dismissed on this basis in 2016/2017, representing just over 1.3% of all complaints.[12] However, some 4,131 of these complaints related to PPI, with a footnote suggesting that many complainants were complaining about PPI policies that did not exist. Only 76 non-PPI complaints were dismissed on this basis.

---

7 *R (Heather Moor & Edgecomb) v FOS* [2008] EWCA Civ 643 at [35-36].

8 DISP 3.3.1R.

9 *R (Heather Moor & Edgecomb) v FOS* [2008] EWCA Civ 643 at [47].

10 There is nothing in DISP 3.3 to limit the time at which the powers can be used and the ability of the FOS to dismiss complaints 'at any stage' is stated in the Glossary definition of 'Chargeable Case'.

11 DISP 3.3.4A(1).

12 Annual activity report 2016/2017. There were a total of 312,159 complaints in that year.

Apart from the comment about the non-existence of PPI policies, the FOS does not provide guidance on what will be seen as frivolous or vexatious.[13] However, it seems to us that the following types of complaint may qualify as frivolous or vexatious:

1. Where the complainant has not been inconvenienced and will suffer no loss as a result of the actions complained about.
2. Very regular complaints from the same complainant about the same respondent, in relation to minor matters, such that the effect is to harass the respondent.
3. Complaints which have the clear intention of harassing the respondent by reason of the respondent's obligation to pay case fees irrespective of the outcome (see Chapter 12).
4. Claims with no basis at all, such as the non-existent PPI policy cases.

It is unclear whether a complaint without any reasonable prospects of success could be said to be vexatious on that ground alone (i.e. where there is no doubt that financial services were provided, but the FOS immediately concludes that the respondent did nothing wrong). For complaints prior to 9 July 2015, that was an independent ground for dismissing a claim,[14] but it was deleted for later complaints.

The DISP rules do not provide for the respondent making representations in respect of summary dismissal, but it is easy to think of examples where it would be appropriate for the respondent to make such submissions. For example, if the complainant had indicated to the respondent that a complaint would be made as a form of blackmail (knowing that a

---

13 In response to a Freedom of Information request, the FOS stated in 2014 that its 'Knowledge and Information Toolkit' does not include notes on frivolous or vexatious complaints:
https://ico.org.uk/media/action-weve-taken/decision-notices/2014/1008586/fs_50500980.pdf

14 DISP 3.3.4R.

case fee would be payable by the respondent), then the respondent should be entitled to provide evidence of that fact to the FOS.

Complaint dealt with by a comparable ADR entity

If a complaint has already been dealt with by a comparable 'ADR entity', then the claim may be dismissed.[15]

This ground for dismissing a claim is based on the ADR Directive.[16] The European Commission publishes a list of ADR entities,[17] though there does not appear to be any mechanism for the FOS to find out about previous decisions by another ADR entity.

The FOS's statistics suggest that 235 complaints were dismissed on this basis in 2016/2017.[18]

Matters subject to litigation

Where a court has already ruled upon the merits of a dispute, the FOS has the power to dismiss the claim.[19] Whilst it is acceptable for a complainant to attempt a FOS complaint first, before turning to litigation, it is generally not acceptable to go through the court process and then complain to the FOS and it would be a rare case that the FOS was willing to consider despite the court having given a decision on the merits.

According to the FOS's annual activity report for 2016/2017, 116 complaints were dismissed on this basis.

---

15 DISP 3.3.4A (2).

16 Directive 2013/11/EU.

17 https://ec.europa.eu/consumers/odr/main/?event=main.adr.show2.

18 Annual activity report 2016/2017.

19 DISP 3.3.4A (3).

Court proceedings currently under way

The FOS may also refuse to consider a complaint if court proceedings are on foot, and have not been stayed for consideration by the FOS.[20] We consider this situation from the perspective of the court proceeding in Chapter 16. It is up to the parties or the court whether to stay court proceedings, but if they are not stayed, then the FOS may dismiss the complaint.

According to the FOS's annual activity report for 2016/2017, 57 complaints were dismissed on this basis.

An attempt was made in *R (Westcott Financial Services Ltd) v FOS* [2014] EWHC 3972 (Admin) to argue that the FOS should also stay complaints where similar court proceedings were under way. Importantly, the relevant court proceedings did not involve the specific complainants, and were effectively test cases of similar but not identical facts. The FOS refused to stay the claims, and this approach was upheld by the court. On the other hand, in the context of court proceedings, disciplinary proceedings and other enquiries, the FOS did indicate in 2005 that it was not willing to consider particular types of complaints in relation to Equitable Life.[21]

In fact, we question whether the FOS would have had the ability, let alone the obligation, to stay proceedings in these circumstances. The DISP rules only refer to dismissal of the complaints where the subject matter of the complaints has been or is the subject of court proceedings but, as the complainants in *Westcott* were not parties to any court action, the rule was inapplicable. No other rule is cited in *Westcott* as a basis for the staying the complaints.

20 DISP 3.3.4A (4).

21 http://www.financial-ombudsman.org.uk/faq/pdf/Equitable_Penrose-related_decision.pdf

Impairment of the operation of the FOS

The final ground on which a complaint can be dismissed is where it would '*seriously impair the effective operation*' of the FOS.[22] This appears to be something of a catch-all for other complaints that the FOS dismisses without consideration of the merits. Importantly, though, a deluge of complaints in a particular area does not appear to be sufficient to prevent the FOS considering such complaints under this rule. The FOS is well used to dealing with widespread complaints, and in appropriate cases has set up bespoke procedures to deal with them.

This criterion is then expanded upon by DISP 3.3.4B G, which lists a number of specific situations where complaints may be dismissed, considered in turn below.

According to the FOS's annual activity report for 2016/2017, 2,602 complaints were dismissed under this heading.

Complaint better dealt with by a court

The FOS may dismiss a case if it considers that it is more appropriate for a court or a comparable ADR entity.[23] This should be distinguished from the FOS's ability to refer test cases to the court or other ADR entities (discussed below) though the two issues are obviously closely linked.

Some guidance on the FOS's approach to this rule may be gleaned from a decision dated 22 March 2005 in relation to various complaints that relied upon findings made by Lord Penrose in respect of Equitable Life products.[24] The FOS decided that it was not an appropriate forum to determine such complaints, noting that there was a possibility of 'stalemate' if FOS decisions overlapped with the FSA's regulatory powers or the decisions were challenged. In the setting of other court

22 DISP 3.3.4AR (4).

23 DISP 3.3.4BG (1).

24 http://www.financial-ombudsman.org.uk/faq/pdf/Equitable_Penrose-related_decision.pdf

and disciplinary proceedings currently underway, and potentially wide implications of any FOS decision on the issues, the FOS decided that it would be more suitable for the complaints to be dealt with by a court.

In *R (Chancery Tax (UK) LLP) v FOS* [2015] EWHC 407 (Admin), the court referred to a final decision in which it was said that the FOS does not usually dismiss cases purely based on the amount in dispute.[25]

However, the FOS has considerable discretion in deciding whether to dismiss claims as more suitable for the court, and in practice it does refuse to consider large complaints on the basis that they would be better considered in court proceedings.

From experience, another factor that the FOS may take into account is the fact that the complaint includes allegations of fraud, or other difficult issues which require cross-examination in court. Although the FOS has jurisdiction to allow oral hearings (see Chapter 10), some cases can only fairly be resolved under oath and with full disclosure from both parties.

Complaint previously determined

A complaint may be dismissed on the basis that the FOS has already considered it or excluded it, unless '*material new evidence to affect the outcome has subsequently become available*'.[26] Accordingly, this provision applies where the FOS has previously decided the complaint, and allows the FOS to reconsider the complaint again.

This provision was considered in *R (Cook) v FOS* [2009] EWHC 426 (Admin), where it was accepted that the FOS should only accept such new evidence if it could not with reasonable diligence have been obtained at the time of the original complaint.[27] On the facts of that case, the complainants sought to rely on an expert report as the new evidence, but the court agreed with the FOS's position that the com-

25 At [44].

26 DISP 3.3.4AR(5) and 3.3.4BG(3).

27 At [35-37].

plainants could have obtained that report at the time of the original complaint.

The *Cook* case also left open a difficult question: where the previous complaint led to a final decision, accepted by the complainants, can the FOS reconsider the complaint based on new evidence? Given that such a final decision becomes binding on both the complainant and the respondent, the FOS's view in *Cook* was that the complaint could not be reconsidered.

It will probably be easier for a complainant to resubmit a complaint if the first complaint was summarily dismissed than if it was determined by a final decision.

Referring disputes to other complaints schemes or the court

The rules provide for the FOS to refer complaints elsewhere in only two circumstances.

The first circumstance is that the FOS considers that another complaints scheme might be more suitable, and the complainant consents to the referral.[28] For example, a complainant might be making a complaint about their pension arrangements, and it is possible that the Pensions Ombudsman might be more suitable. In fact, the FOS has agreed a memorandum of understanding with the Pensions Ombudsman,[29] which explains that the issues that each service will take into account when deciding whether to refer a complaint to the other include:

1. The potential redress and the limits applicable to each service, if the other service has the ability to make greater awards.

2. The applicable time limits for each service, such that a complaint might be out of time with the FOS but in time for the Pensions Ombudsman.

---

28 DISP 3.4.1R.

29 http://www.financial-ombudsman.org.uk/assets/pdf/2017-12-01-MoU-between-The%20Pensions-Ombudsman-and-the-Financial-Ombudsman-Service.pdf

3. If a complaint relates to multiple respondents and the FOS only has jurisdiction over one respondent whereas the Pensions Ombudsman has jurisdiction over both respondents.

If a complainant refuses the transfer, the memorandum of understanding suggests that the FOS might decide to dismiss the complaint in accordance with its usual powers. In other words, it may dismiss the complaint under the rules described above.

Though it is not apparent in the rules, the FOS may also refer complaints to the Pensions Ombudsman even without the complainant's consent, if the FOS concludes that it does not have jurisdiction but that the Pensions Ombudsman might be able to consider the complaint.[30]

The second circumstance in which the FOS will consider referring a case is where the complaint could usefully be considered by the courts, as a test case. Again, this can only happen with the complainant's consent. We consider this in greater detail in Chapter 16.[31]

30 Pursuant to the memorandum of understanding dated 1 December 2017.

31 DISP 3.4.2R. Further guidance on the factors that the FOS will take into account are at DISP 3.4.3G.

CHAPTER NINE
FACT FINDING

The rules state that an ombudsman will give both parties an opportunity to make representations, before proceeding to a decision.[1] In reality, much of the fact finding is conducted by adjudicators, before being considered by ombudsmen.

Typically, the FOS will contact the parties and seek information on specific issues. This is often by email, and is an iterative process: the FOS may make repeated requests for evidence and seek explanations of issues that arise from that evidence. The FOS is entitled to look beyond the complaint itself and to look more widely at the available evidence.[2]

In doing so, the FOS is not limited in the type of evidence it can consider. Unlike litigation, there are no 'rules of evidence' and the rules states explicitly that the FOS may exclude evidence that a court would accept, or include evidence that would not be admissible in court.[3]

This means that there is no need for oaths, or formal witness statements, and the FOS will accept evidence provided by email or by any reasonable means.

Nevertheless, any party to a FOS complaint should do their best to provide contemporaneous documentary evidence to support their case. Particularly given the extreme rarity of oral hearings (see Chapter 10), the FOS will often accept such documents and written evidence at face value.

Expert evidence

Parties can put forward expert evidence in support of their case, but that is the exception rather than the norm. The FOS will not necessarily

---

1 DISP 3.5.4R.

2 *R (Full Circle Asset Management Ltd) v FOS* [2017] EWHC 323 (Admin) at [54].

3 DISP 3.5.9R (1).

accept such evidence, and may conclude that the respondent acted negligently even if the respondent obtains an expert report supporting its conduct.[4] If a party does wish to rely on an expert's report, however, it must do so before the final decision is issued. Attempts to do so at a later date will likely be too late.[5]

Likewise, a respondent can put forward an opinion from counsel,[6] but the FOS is not bound to agree with it and can, in any event, reach a conclusion that is fair and reasonable, and contrary to the strict legal position (see Chapter 11).

Communications from the FOS

The FOS may also communicate with parties in a way that would not be appropriate by a judge in litigation. For example, there is no problem with the FOS enquiring with a respondent whether it intends to rely on a time-bar where the respondent has not raised the issue itself.[7]

The rules also allow the FOS to receive information on a confidential basis, so that it is not disclosed to the other party, or only in redacted form.[8] Whilst that may well be appropriate for some evidence, there may be issues with this approach if the information is crucial to the FOS's decision and is not disclosed. As we discuss in Chapter 17, the FOS is required to comply with the rules of natural justice and this will typically require a party to understand and be able to respond to the evidence relied upon by the FOS.

---

4 *R (Heather Moor & Edgecomb) v FOS* [2008] EWCA Civ 642 at [56].

5 *R (Cook) v FOS* [2009] EWHC 426 (Admin) and *R (Walker) v FOS* [2013] NIQB 12 at [22].

6 As in *R (IFG Financial Services Ltd) v FOS* [2005] EWHC 1153 (Admin).

7 *R (Ropaigealach) v FOS* [2005] EWCA Civ 269 at [15]

8 DISP 3.5.9R (2).

Directions from the FOS

The FOS will usually set down time limits for the provision of evidence,[9] and a failure by a complainant to provide the evidence in time can lead to the FOS treating the complaint as withdrawn.[10] In fact, the FOS is often amenable to requests for more time to provide information, and it would be surprising for a single failure to meet a deadline to lead to such a result.

The FOS also has the power, under s. 231 of FSMA, to require either party to a complaint to provide information and documents. If that party does not provide the documents, then under s. 232 of FSMA the FOS may certify that fact to the High Court, and the party can be held in contempt of court if there is no reasonable excuse for withholding the information/documents. There are no reported cases in which the FOS has taken this step, and it is likely that it would only do so in extreme cases.

Particularly where it is the respondent that fails to provide information, it is more likely that the FOS would draw inferences from the lack of evidence and reach negative findings.[11] Given that respondents also have a duty to co-operate with the FOS,[12] there may also be regulatory consequences for refusing to provide information when requested.

The FOS's inquisitorial approach

Where the evidence suggests that the complaint has been formulated incorrectly, or misses the real problem, the FOS may consider a different formulation of the complaint. The FOS may also consider further evidence, not provided by the parties. However, if it does so, the FOS should make it clear to both parties before reaching a final decision. In practice, this will normally be achieved through the pro-

9 DISP 3.5.13R.

10 DISP 3.5.9R (4) and DISP 3.5.15R.

11 DISP 3.5.9R (4).

12 DISP 1.4.4R.

vision of the adjudicator's findings and the ombudsman's provisional decision.[13]

Provisional and final decisions

Before an ombudsman issues a final decision, the rules require that both parties be sent a provisional decision.[14]

They are, as the name suggests, an expression by the ombudsman of factual findings, and the decision that the ombudsman proposes to make. They are provided to the parties for comment, and often lead to the provision of further evidence or submissions by one party or the other, aimed at correcting what they see as the ombudsman's mistakes. Accordingly, the provisional decision should be seen as furthering the fact finding process, and to ensure that the parties have an opportunity to make submissions on the ombudsman's proposed approach.

They also serve a protecting purpose for the FOS: because the parties can see what the ombudsman is thinking, and what they are taking into account, it is hard to argue in a judicial review that either party was unaware of the case that they were expected to meet, prior to the final decision. This is discussed in Chapter 17.

The final decision should be supported by sufficient reasons that the parties can understand why the ombudsman reached his/her conclusions. However, the requirement is not as high as it would be for a judgment in court. Given the informal nature of FOS complaints, it will be sufficient if the ombudsman approaches matters on a common sense basis, and it is not required to address every argument put forward by the parties, as long as the conclusion is clear.[15]

As to the awards that the FOS may make, see Chapter 13.

13 See *R (Green) v FOS* [2003] EWHC 338 (Admin) at [49-52] and R (Full Circle Asset Management) v FOS [2017] EWHC 323 (Admin) at [57].

14 DISP 3.5.4R refers to 'provisional assessment', but they are more normally referred to as provisional decisions.

15 *R (Garrison Investment Analysis) v FOS* [2006] EWHC 2466 (Admin) at [5].

CHAPTER TEN
ORAL HEARINGS

The current DISP rules relating to oral hearings state:

> *'If the Ombudsman considers that the complaint can be fairly determined without convening a hearing, he will determine the complaint. If not, he will invite the parties to take part in a hearing. A hearing may be held by any means which the Ombudsman considers appropriate in the circumstances, including by telephone. No hearing will be held after the Ombudsman has determined the complaint....*
>
> *In deciding whether there should be a hearing and, if so, whether it should be in public or private, the Ombudsman will have regard to the provisions of the European Convention on Human Rights.'*[1]

The circumstances relevant to whether the FOS should hold oral hearings have been considered a number of times by the courts, from which we draw the following propositions:

1. The European Convention on Human Rights does not contain an absolute right to an oral hearing: the overarching principle is one of fairness.[2]

2. Nevertheless, there may be cases in which fairness demands that an oral hearing take place.[3]

3. Where the fair determination of the complaint requires investigation of what was said at meetings, and those facts are contested, fairness may require an oral hearing.[4] Even then, it

---

1 DISP 3.5.5R and DISP 3.5.7G.

2 *Jussila v Finland* (2006) 45 EHRR 892, quoted in *R (Heather Moor & Edgecomb) v FOS* [2008] EWCA Civ 642 at [64].

3 *R (Heather Moor & Edgecomb) v FOS* [2009] EWHC 2701 (Admin) at [10].

4 *R (Heather Moor & Edgecomb) v FOS* [2008] EWCA Civ 642 at [58].

may be sufficient to test the accuracy of the complainant's evidence in writing in the interests of efficiency and economy.[5]

4. The FOS is entitled to take a common sense view of matters such as causation without hearing evidence from the complainant. For example, there will usually be no need for an oral hearing to test whether a complainant relied upon advice received from a financial advisor: it will usually be fair to presume reliance.[6]

5. Likewise, if the FOS takes the view that bad advice was given, then it will not be necessary to investigate precisely what was said as part of that bad advice.[7]

6. The FOS is also entitled to conclude that an oral hearing is unlikely to resolve disputed issues of fact, where the oral hearing would take place so long after the relevant meeting that it is unlikely to produce useful evidence.[8]

As a more general point, it should be noted there is no reported decision in which a FOS decision has been quashed by reason of the lack of an oral hearing.

We also searched for the phrase 'oral hearing' on the database of FOS decisions. Out of 55 decisions listed, it appears that no hearings were listed: in each case, the ombudsman reported that a hearing had been requested or at least mentioned by one of the parties, but none were held.

Despite their apparent rarity, the FOS has produced 'a quick guide to hearings', which sets out the approach that it will take to hearings.[9] It

5 *R (Heather Moor & Edgecomb) v FOS* [2008] EWCA Civ 642 at [65].

6 *R (Heather Moor & Edgecomb) v FOS* [2008] EWCA Civ 642 at [60].

7 *R (Heather Moor & Edgecomb) v FOS* [2009] EWHC 2701 (Admin) at [13]. Similar reasoning was used in *R (Calland) v FOS* [2013] EWHC 1327 (Admin) at [113], where an advisor disputed the alleged advice he had given, but it was common ground that he had in fact given advice.

8 *R (Calland) v FOS* [2013] EWHC 1327 (Admin) at [114].

provides little concrete guidance as to the type of situation in which a hearing will be held, beyond situations where '*we think a hearing will help resolve issues that are relevant.*'

If a hearing is to take place:

1. It will occur after the adjudicator has issued their recommendations and before the ombudsman issues a final decision.

2. It will usually take place in the FOS's offices in London.

3. Questions will be put by the ombudsman. Direct cross-examination by one party of another is unlikely to be allowed.

4. Lawyers are discouraged, and if a respondent intends to attend with its legal representatives, the FOS may invite the respondent to pay for representatives for the complainant as well.

9 http://www.financial-ombudsman.org.uk/publications/technical_notes/QG3-hearings.pdf

CHAPTER ELEVEN
DETERMINING THE COMPLAINT: THE FOS'S 'FAIR AND REASONABLE' APPROACH

This chapter focuses on the FOS's approach to resolving complaints.

Given the very wide variety of complaints seen by the FOS, it is not possible to set out all of the factors that will play a part in the eventual outcome, but the overall approach of the FOS is clear. As set out in FSMA, s. 228(2): '*A complaint is to be determined by reference to what is, in the opinion of the ombudsman, fair and reasonable in all the circumstances of the case.*'[1]

This is supplemented by DISP 3.6.4R:

> '*In considering what is fair and reasonable in all the circumstances of the case, the Ombudsman will take into account: (1) relevant: (a) law and regulations; (b) regulators' rules, guidance and standards; (c) codes of practice; and (2) (where appropriate) what he considers to have been good industry practice at the relevant time.*'

When considering a complaint, and what is fair and reasonable, the FOS is not merely reviewing the respondent's decisions to consider whether it was within a range of reasonable outcomes. Instead, the FOS makes its own assessment of what is fair and reasonable on the facts of the case.[2]

Application of the law

One of the innovations of the FOS is that the FOS is not required to apply English law.[3] Instead, as DISP 3.6.4R states, the Ombudsman will take English law into account, along with other relevant rules and

---

1 Repeated in DISP 3.6.1R.

2 *R (Aviva Life and Pensions (UK) Ltd) v FOS* [2017] EWHC 352 (Admin) at [58].

standards and good industry practice. It follows that a case can succeed before the FOS which would fail if considered by the court.

It has been suggested that this means that the FOS can act unpredictably and arbitrarily, and so breaches the rule of law. The Court of Appeal rejected that argument in *R (Heather Moor & Edgecomb) v FOS* [2008] EWCA Civ 642, holding that there is sufficient certainty as to outcome. It held that that the FOS should apply the relevant law, regulations, rules etc. save in exceptional circumstances and, even then, the FOS is required to address the relevant law and explain why it is not being applied.[4]

However, the matter is not closed. In a 'postscript' in *R (Aviva Life and Pensions (UK) Ltd) v FOS* [2017] EWHC 352 (Admin), Jay J expressed concerns about the ability of the FOS to reach conclusions that would be rejected by a court. Why, he asked, should the FOS be allowed to reject a conclusion that the courts had decided is just?

For the time being, at least, these are interesting academic questions but the law is clear. As long as the FOS explains why it is not following the law, it may depart from it. The cases suggest that the FOS will not be required to go into significant detail as to why the law is not being followed. In *R (IFG Financial Services Ltd) v FOS* [2005] EWHC 1153 (Admin), the respondent firm had obtained leading counsel's opinion as to the law of causation. The FOS accepted that the opinion was an accurate statement of the law, but it did not apply it. The court upheld the decision, stating that it is sufficient for the FOS ombudsman to set out what he considers to be fair and reasonable in the circumstances.[5]

Normally, the only basis upon which such conclusions could be challenged is if the FOS acted irrationally (see Chapter 17).

---

3 Confirmed in *R (Heather Moor & Edgecomb) v FOS* [2008] EWCA Civ 642 at [36].

4 *R (Heather Moor & Edgecomb) v FOS* [2008] EWCA Civ 642 at [49]. Also see Aviva v FOS [2017] EWHC 352 (Admin) at [59].

5 See paragraph 90.

Application of the FCA Rules

When reaching its conclusions, the FOS will accord significant weight to the FCA Rules, including the high level 'Principles'.[6] Indeed, the FOS may find against a respondent based on the Principles, even if the respondent otherwise complied with all of the specific rules in the FCA Handbook.[7] This is despite the fact that the breach of a Principle would not in itself give rise to a cause of action in law.

As above, if the FOS concludes that the respondent has acted unreasonably, despite following all specific FCA Rules on the matter, it is incumbent on the FOS to provide sufficient reasons to explain why it does so.[8]

Where the FCA has made relevant findings

There may be cases in which the FCA has considered some of the specific issues that are part of the complaint before the FOS. This is particularly likely where the FCA has concluded that there are systemic problems in an area of financial services (such as PPI). There can be no doubt that the FOS is entitled to take those findings into account when reaching its own decisions.

On the other hand, the FOS will not always dismiss a complaint just because the FCA has looked into the same or similar matter and concluded that there is not a significant problem. This was the position in *R (Full Circle Asset Management Ltd) v FOS* [2017] EWHC 323 (Admin), where the FCA had expressed a view on the riskiness of an investment portfolio. Without disagreeing with that conclusion, the FOS was still entitled to conclude that the portfolio was inappropriate for the requirements of an individual investor.

---

6 *R (British Bankers Association) v FSA* [2011] EWHC 999 (Admin) at [75-78].

7 *R (British Bankers Association) v FSA* [2011] EWHC 999 (Admin) at [184].

8 *R (British Bankers Association) v FSA* [2011] EWHC 999 (Admin) at [186].

Use of an ombudsman's own knowledge

DISP 3.6.4R, together with the inquisitorial role of the FOS,[9] means that a decision may be based on the ombudsman's personal knowledge and experience of the financial services industry.[10]

The courts recognise that this gives rise to the risk that an ombudsman may use hindsight, particularly when change in an area of the industry has been rapid and unexpected. It has been suggested that the use of personal experience by an ombudsman should depend on the type of question in issue: if the matter is straightforward and uncontroversial, then the ombudsman can certainly proceed based on experience, but there should be greater circumspection if the matter is more complicated. [11]

That said, even if a FOS decision does rest on the personal experience of complicated matters, it will still be difficult to overturn the decision, given the difficulties in judicially reviewing the FOS: see Chapter 17.

---

9 See Chapter 7.

10 *R (Williams) v FOS* [2008] EWHC 2142 (Admin) at [26].

11 *R (Williams) v FOS* [2008] EWHC 2142 (Admin) at [45].

CHAPTER TWELVE
PAYING FOR THE COMPLAINT

Complainants to the FOS are not required to pay anything to bring their complaint. Instead, the FOS as a whole is paid for by the financial services industry through levies and case fees.[1]

This book does not consider the intricacies of the levies and the fees but readers may be interested the overall structure of the fees paid per complaint.

Most complaints to the FOS are 'chargeable cases', meaning that the respondent may be required to pay for it, depending on how many complaints have been made about that respondent in the same financial year or whether the respondent can benefit from an exemption.[2] The same fees apply to respondents under the compulsory jurisdiction and voluntary jurisdiction.[3]

Chargeable cases include any complaint, except those where:[4]

1. The FOS decides that the complaint should not proceed because the complainant is not an eligible complainant, because the complaint falls outside the FOS's jurisdiction, or because the complaint should be dismissed without considering its merits (see Chapter 8).

2. At a later stage, the FOS concludes that complaint should be dismissed as frivolous or vexatious (also see Chapter 8).

---

1 As envisaged by FSMA, s. 234.

2 E.g. cash plan health providers and small friendly providers: FEES 5.5B.3R and 5.5B.4G.

3 FEES 5.5B.2G.

4 From the Glossary definition of Chargeable Case within the FCA Handbook.

3. The complaint has already been dealt with by the respondent under the terms of a consumer redress scheme.

All complaints are chargeable unless they fall within the exceptions above.

At the time of writing, the first 25 chargeable complaints about a respondent within a financial year are 'free' to that respondent, and the FOS starts charging for each case after that, at a cost of £550.[5] The rules also provide for supplementary case fees, relating to PPI complaints,[6] and special case fees, being additional fees paid by large banking and insurance respondents.[7]

Respondents have to pay for chargeable cases whether the complaint is successful or not. Whilst some might see this as unfair, the courts have confirmed the validity of the charges.[8]

---

5 FEES 5 Annex 3R, Part 1.

6 FEES 5.5B17-19, and FEES 5 Annex 3R, Part 2.

7 FEES 5.5B20-23 and Fees 5 Annex 3R, Part 3.

8 *R (Heather Moor & Edgecomb) v FOS* [2008] EWCA Civ 643.

CHAPTER THIRTEEN
FOS AWARDS

This chapter outlines the powers which the FOS has to make awards in favour of complainants who have been successful.

As regards the compulsory jurisdiction, the FOS's powers are contained in s.229 (2) of FSMA. The determination may include an award against the respondent of such amount as the FOS considers 'fair compensation' for 'loss and damage'. It can also include a direction that the respondent takes 'such steps' in relation to the complainant as the FOS considers just and appropriate.

The effect of these provisions is that the FOS has the power, in relation to the compulsory jurisdiction, to make both monetary awards and also order the taking of other steps. It matters not whether the court would have the power to make an order in those terms.

DISP 4.2.4R provides that the FOS has the same powers to make determinations and awards under the voluntary jurisdiction as it has under the compulsory jurisdiction. FOS determinations, if accepted by the complainant in time, will be binding on the VJ Participant and can be enforced in court.

As we shall also see, the FOS also has certain powers in relation to the award of costs.

Monetary awards

In respect of what losses can an award be made?

DISP 3.7.2R allows the FOS to award compensation for:

1. Financial loss, which can include consequential loss or prospective loss.

2. Pain and suffering.

3. Damage to reputation.

4. Distress or inconvenience.

The position is slightly different for complaints in respect of consumer redress schemes, under FSMA s. 404B. In such cases, the FOS has jurisdiction to make a money award of such amount as the FOS determines the respondent should make or should have made to the complainant.[1] In essence, the FOS operates as an appeal mechanism from the consumer redress scheme, and if the complaint is upheld the FOS will usually make whatever money award the complainant should have been awarded under the redress scheme.

How are monetary awards calculated?

A monetary award can be made in such amount as the FOS considers fair compensation for loss or damage suffered by the complainant. The award can compensate for financial loss or any other loss or damage of a 'specified kind'.[2] Although not explicitly stated, it appears that these 'specified kinds' of losses are those referred to above, set out in DISP 3.7.2R.

Either way, the primary aim of a monetary award is that it has to be compensatory. The FOS's website confirms that, if a complaint is upheld, its aim generally will be to put the complainant in the position they would have been in if the problem had not happened.[3]

But the FOS is not required to apply the same principles as a court would when working out what compensation should be paid. The award has to be for what the FOS considers 'fair compensation' (implying some degree of subjectivity), subject to the limits of reasonableness and what can be challenged on a judicial review.[4]

1 DISP 3.7.2AG.

2 FSMA, s.229(2) and (3).

3 See http://www.financial-ombudsman.org/publications/technical_notes/compensation-for-investment-loss.htm.

For more information on challenges by judicial review, see Chapter 17. As explained in that chapter, such challenges are rarely successful. So, in *R (IFG Financial Services Ltd) v FOS* [2005] EWHC 1153 (Admin), the court rejected a challenge to a FOS decision where the FOS had essentially refused to apply orthodox principles about remoteness of damages[5] and scope of liability[6] when assessing the complainants' damages. The FOS had referred to the relevant principles when coming to its determination, but simply decided that it was not fair and reasonable to apply them. The mere fact this result differed from that which would follow from a strict application of English law was not enough to result in a successful challenge.

In terms of the reasons that the FOS needed to give when reaching its conclusions as to how damages should be calculated, all that was required on the facts of *IFG* was that the FOS made clear what it thought to be fair and reasonable in the circumstances.[7]

Compensation for pecuniary losses

Often, the FOS may ask a respondent to compensate a complainant for an investment loss or being deprived of the use of their money. The former will be awarded where, for instance, the complainant is found to have purchased an unsuitable product. Where that is so, the FOS will normally award compensation based on what would have happened to

---

4 e.g. *R (IFG Financial Services Ltd) v FOS* [2005] EWHC 1153 (Admin) at paragraphs [17] *et seq.*

5 i.e. the notion that, in order to be recoverable, a loss must be reasonably foreseeable.

6 See *South Australia Asset Management Corp v York Montague Ltd* [1997] AC 191.

7 At [90].

the complainant's money if the investment had not been made.[8] In working that out, there will usually be one of three alternatives.[9]

First, the complainant would have left their money where it was. In these situations, the FOS will usually calculate compensation based on what the complainant would have had if they had not moved their money, compared with the value of the investment purchased by the complainant.

Secondly, the complainant would have put their money into a specific, alternative investment. Obviously there will need to be evidence to support the contention that the complainant would have taken out the alternative investment. Perhaps the strongest evidence of that will be derived from the discussions when the original investment was taking place. If there was consideration of an alternative investment and the FOS has sufficient evidence to conclude that the complainant would have made that investment instead, the FOS will assess the difference between the value of the mis-sold investment and the alternative investment.[10]

Thirdly, the complainant would have put their money elsewhere, but it is not clear where. Here, the FOS will simply do the best it can, and identify the broad 'qualities' the alternative investment wold have had, reflecting what the FOS thinks overall might have been invested. The FOS will then normally tell the business to work out the difference between the complainant's financial position in respect of the mis-sold investment and a benchmark reflecting the qualities of the alternative. On its website, the FOS gives examples of stockmarket indices, deposit rates or a combination, albeit that '*the particular circumstances involved*'

8 See http://www.financial-ombudsman.org/publications/technical_notes/compensation-for-investment-loss.htm under the heading "*compensation for investment loss*". Also see: http://www.financial-ombudsman.org/publications/technical_notes/calculating-comp-investment-complaint.html.

9 *Ibid.*

10 See http://www.financial-ombudsman.org/publications/technical_notes/calculating-comp-investment-complaint.html under the heading "*what if can reasonably identify the investments the consumer would have taken out?*".

may require alternatives, such as the Bank of England Base Rate (which the FOS says may be used in cases where it is not possible to identify a suitable benchmark).[11]

The FOS's own guidance makes clear that the amount of risk the complainant would have taken on is important and will have a bearing on the benchmark measures that may be used.[12]

For instance, if the complainant is considered to have wanted '*to achieve a reasonable return and some flexibility with their investment but did not want to risk their capital*', the FOS will usually require the respondent to compare the consumer's current position with what their position would have been if the return had matched the average rate for a one year fixed rate bond. This appears to be a good example of how the FOS will depart from the strict legal principles that would be applied by a court. A court might require the complainant to prove what alternative investment would have been taken out. The FOS does not require the complainant to do so. The FOS's approach is to reflect broadly the '*sort of investment return a consumer could have obtained with little risk to capital*'.[13]

Complainants comfortable with more risk might have their awards assessed by reference to stock markets such as the FTSE UK Private Investors Income total return index.[14]

---

11 *Ibid* and http://www.financial-ombudsman.org/publications/technical_notes/calculating-comp-investment-complaint.html under the heading "*what if we think the consumer would have invested differently – but we can't say what exactly they would have done differently?*". Note that the FOS normally assumes the benchmark rates reflect what the consumer would have made net of charges, so account will not be made for these, but the calculations will need to take into account things like capital withdrawals and income payments

12 http://www.financial-ombudsman.org/publications/technical_notes/calculating-comp-investment-complaint.html under the heading "*what if we think the consumer would have invested differently – but we can't say what exactly they would have done differently?*".

13 *Ibid.*

14 *Ibid.*

Complainants that fall in between these two risk profiles will have their awards assessed using a starting point of a 50:50 combination.[15] This presumably can be changed depending on the amount of risk the complainant would have been willing to undertake.

The respondent may also be ordered to repay the fees it charged for advice if, as part of the steps which the complainant needs to take to put matters right, they will have to pay further fees. Simple interest will be added to this at a rate of 8%. But no such refund will be given where the respondent has already taken 'appropriate action' to correct a situation without charging a further fee.[16]

Where the complainant no longer has the investment product at the date their award is assessed, the FOS will normally require the respondent to pay: (i) compensation to cover the investment loss from the date the investment was taken out to the date it was disposed of; and (ii) interest from the date of disposal until the date of payment (normally at a rate of 8% simple).[17]

Often, complainants will still hold the investment at the time their award is made. As long as the investment is liquid and its value ascertainable, the value of the continued investment will be taken into account. The complainant may also then keep their investment. Needless to say, should the complainant then suffer further losses on the investment after a FOS award, they will not normally be entitled to seek redress for these losses from the FOS.[18]

However, where the market is illiquid the complainant will not be able to sell the investment and FOS will have the difficulty that '*we can't be sure about what value, if any, the consumer might be able to realise from*

15 *Ibid.*

16 *Ibid.* under the heading "*what if the consumer has to pay an advice fee to put things right?*".

17 *Ibid.* under the heading "*where the consumer no longer has the unsuitable investment*".

18 *Ibid.*

the investment in future'.[19] In this case, the FOS will normally require the investment to be transferred to the business and the complainant will be awarded the full value of their losses. However, this result can be complicated by the FOS's compensatory cap of £150,000 (see below). If the FOS makes a recommendation above the cap, and the respondent does not follow it, then the complainant will be able to keep their investment in addition to the money award. After all, they will not have been properly compensated otherwise.[20]

As an alternative, the FOS may always award compensation on the basis that the investment should be treated as if it were rescinded. This approach usually arises where the complainant has entered into a contract with the respondent which has produced no value for the customer. A typical example might be a PPI policy which has now expired. This will normally involve the respondent repaying the complainant things like premiums that were charged, plus simple interest at 8%.[21]

Compensation for non-pecuniary losses

DISP 3.7.2R allows the FOS to make money awards in respect of certain non-pecuniary losses (pain and suffering, damage to reputation, and distress or inconvenience). The FOS collectively refers to these as awards for 'trouble and upset'.

Often, these types of award will be made when the FOS makes a finding that the complainant has received poor service, but cannot identify any real loss. A court (even if it could find a cause of action) would have only the power to award nominal damages in this situation. The FOS, however, may make an award. Experience suggests that these are typically in the region of a couple of hundred pounds at most, and even then the FOS may just order the respondent to provide a simple

---

19 *Ibid.* under the heading "*what if the investment cannot be sold or surrendered?*".

20 *Ibid.* Note the particular rules concerning pensions.

21 http://www.financial-ombudsman.org/publications/technical_notes/calculating-comp-investment-complaint.html under the heading "*other forms of compensation*"

apology. The FOS would consider anything above £300 as 'significant' compensation; over £1,000 is 'exceptional'.[22]

The FOS takes an expansive view as to what constitutes distress, defining it on its website as '*including embarrassment, anxiety, disappointment, loss of expectation, upset and stress*'. Likewise, inconvenience is said to include '*the time someone's spent and / or effort they've had to go to as a result*' of a mistake.[23]

Awards for this type of loss have the risk of becoming arbitrary. The FOS recognises that the purpose of these awards is not to punish, but rather recognise the '*emotional and practical impact*' of the matters in respect of which a complaint has been made. The FOS is keen to stress that there must be some link between the conduct complained of and the distress.[24] The FOS will ask whether the consumer has acted reasonably, in a way to mitigate the problem.[25] Claims for time spent (that do not give rise to a financial loss) will need to be evidenced.[26]

<u>What form does a monetary award take?</u>

There are two alternatives here. First, the FOS can simply state, as a figure, the amount which it thinks the respondent should pay. For most complaints, and particularly those concerning distress, damage to reputation and other non-pecuniary losses, this is likely to be the form which the award takes. The second possibility is that the FOS specifies a formula by which compensation can be calculated. This is more often used in circumstances where compensation for a mis-sold investment is granted. In these types of case, it will be the duty of the respondent to

---

22 See *Ombudsman News* Issue 71 (August 2008).

23 http://www.financial-ombudsman.org/publications/technical_notes/distress-and-inconvenience.htm

24 http://www.financial-ombudsman.org/publications/technical_notes/distress-and-inconvenience.htm

25 *Ibid.* under the heading "*how should the compensation be paid?*".

26 *Ibid.* under the heading "*do we award compensation for people's time?*"

carry out the relevant calculation. The FOS will not normally check the calculations provided by the respondent.[27]

How much can a monetary award be for?

The monetary awards that the FOS can make are limited by its rules. Currently, awards can be made for a maximum of £150,000.[28] If there are still any complaints in the system that were initiated before 1 January 2012, the cap is £100,000.

Section 404B (5) of FSMA provides that awards in respect of complaints arising out of consumer redress schemes are subject to the same limits.

When judging whether an award exceeds this limit, the FOS is to exclude the interest on the award, any costs awarded, and any interest on costs.[29] Once these further awards are taken into account, the overall award can therefore exceed £150,000.

Many serious financial mis-selling claims will seek losses far in excess of the FOS's statutory limit. At least where a complainant is represented by lawyers, it is questionable whether a claim that is likely to be well above these should even be submitted to the FOS at all, absent peculiar features. Indeed, the FOS itself will normally write to complainants where this is the case so that they can decide whether to continue using the FOS procedures and take legal advice.[30] This is necessary in view of the fact that, as we shall we see, accepting a FOS award will normally preclude a claim in court for the sums in excess of £150,000.

---

27 http://www.financial-ombudsman.org/publications/technical_notes/calculating-comp-investment-complaint.html under the heading "*will the ombudsman check that compensation calculations have been carried out correctly*". Sample calculations are available on the FOS's website.

28 DISP 3.7.4R and FSMA, s.229.

29 DISP 3.7.5G.

30 See http://www.financial-ombudsman.org.uk/publications/technical_notes/compensation.html under the heading "*what if we think that fair compensation will be more than the maximum limit of £150,000*".

The FOS may also dismiss complaints as being unsuitable for its procedures (see Chapter 8).[31]

Nevertheless, where the FOS considers that fair compensation would require a payment in excess of £150,000, it may require payment of £150,000 and 'recommend' that the respondent pay a larger sum.[32] However, it will be for the respondent to decide whether to follow this recommendation and to the extent that the award exceeds £150,000, it cannot be enforced in the courts.

Given the limits on monetary awards, it is quite normal for complainants to submit multiple complaints about very similar issues. An investor who complains that she was advised to invest in Investment X, Investment Y and Investment Z, all of which were unsuitable, may therefore submit three complaints. The rules allow the FOS to consider complaints relating to 'connected circumstances' together, and make a monetary award in respect of each complaint.[33] It follows that a complainant can be awarded multiples of the maximum monetary award in appropriate circumstances. There is little guidance on when it is appropriate to 'split' complaints in this way, but anecdotally it has been suggested that the FOS actively encourages this approach.

<u>Interest</u>

The FOS has the power to order the payment of interest, at a rate and from a date set by the FOS. [34]

For complaints in respect of consumer redress schemes, the FOS has the power to order that interest is payable on any amount which is not paid by the date specified in the award for payment.[35]

---

31 DISP 3.3.4AR (5) and 3.3.4BG (1).

32 FSMA, s.229 (5) and DISP 3.7.6G. This power applies to the voluntary jurisdiction as well.

33 DISP 3.5.3G.

34 DISP 3.7.1R (2) and DISP 3.7.8R.

35 DISP 3.7.8AG.

The FOS states that the amount of interest will need to be calculated by reference to each case.[36] The aim is of course to put a complainant in the position which they would have been in but for the conduct complained of. The FOS considers that 'in many cases' this will be 8% simple interest per year from the date of the loss. [37]

Interest will continue to run until the date of payment. This is inherent in the fact that the award will provide for interest to be payable from a specified date, but no end-date for the interest is specified.

Obviously, the FOS will need to be astute to ensure that an award of interest does not overlap with the relief given in their main monetary award. For many financial mis-selling claims, this will mean that an award of 8% interest is not appropriate, because the award will take into account the value of the investments that the complainant should have at the date of the award. Interest in these circumstances would amount to double recovery.

Costs

The FOS has the power to make awards in respect of costs.[38]

Whilst many of the complainants before the FOS will not have representation or professional advisers assisting them, and such awards are unlikely to be common,[39] for more serious or high value cases, it will be reasonable for assistance of some description to be obtained. Where that is so, the FOS will make an award in such amount as it considers to be fair, to cover some or all of the costs that were reasonably incurred by the complainant. Interest may also be ordered to be paid on costs.[40]

---

36 See http://www.financial-ombudsman.org.uk/publications/ombudsman-news/33/awards-33.htm.

37 *Ibid.*

38 DISP 3.7.1R(3). This power is derived from FSMA, s. 230. By s.230 (7), a costs award is enforceable in the same way as other awards for money in accordance with FSMA, Schedule 17, Part II, paragraph 16: see Chapter 15.

39 DISP 3.7.10G.

40 DISP 3.7.9R.

A couple of points are worth noting about these powers. The first is that, as stated, they will not be common or usual. Indeed, if the case really is sufficiently large or complex to justify representation of some description, there may be an argument about whether litigation would have been a more appropriate avenue for the dispute.

Secondly, the FOS only has the power to make awards in respect of a complainant's costs. Respondents are not able to recover their costs. Indeed, this is specifically prohibited by s.230(3) of FSMA.

Thirdly, the costs award can only be in respect of those that were reasonably incurred. This will require an assessment by the FOS. Presumably, similar factors as to those which a court takes into account when assessing costs will be considered. That will include the amount at stake, the complexity of the arguments, the level of fees, and the conduct of the parties (including any offers of reparation that may have been made).

Directions

In addition to its powers to make monetary awards, the FOS can order that a respondent take steps in relation to the complainant which the FOS considers 'just and appropriate'.[41] This is obviously inspired by the court's power to grant injunctions and specific performance. But the rules confirm that the FOS's power to issue directions can be made whether or not a court could order those steps to be taken.[42]

Whilst the usual factors that are taken into account by courts when assessing whether to grant injunctions or specific performance will doubtless, be relevant when assessing what is just and appropriate, the FOS will not be confined in the same way.

A direction may be enforceable by a court by way of an injunction (see Chapter 15).[43]

---

41 DISP 3.7.11R.

42 FSMA, s. 229(2)(b); DISP 3.7.11R.

43 See s.229(9) of FSMA.

However, a direction will not be enforced to the extent that it imposes a cost on the respondent in excess of the £150,000 cap that would apply to monetary awards.[44] Whether an award is a direction or a monetary award will depend on its substance not form. So, if the determination requires the payment of money to the complainant or for his benefit it is a money award.[45]

Where a direction is made which would cost more than £150,000, it will be subject to an implied limitation that compliance is only required up to the cap.[46] One can imagine scenarios where the application of this rule will be very difficult. If an insurance company is directed to make good defects caused by subsidence, for example, it may be unknowable how much the remedial works will cost; would the court issue an injunction requiring the insurance company to start on the works, on the basis that they can stop once their costs hit £150,000? Such issues have not, as far as we are aware, arisen in practice.

Publication of awards

Since 1 April 2013, the FOS has reported most of its determinations on http://www.ombudsman-decisions.org.uk/. It reports all of its decisions, unless it is of the view that publication is inappropriate.[47] These reports are anonymised in respect of the complainant,[48] but bear the name of the respondent against whom the complaint was referred.

The FOS also publishes data about the number of complaints against individual firms, and the number of complaints that are upheld against such firms.

---

44 *Bunney v Burns Anderson PLC* [2007] EWHC 1240 (Ch).

45 *Bunney* at [68].

46 *R (Aviva Life and Pensions (UK) Ltd) v FOS* at [54].

47 DISP 3.6.8G (1).

48 DISP 3.6.8G (2), unless the complainant consents.

CHAPTER FOURTEEN HOW AN AWARD IS ACCEPTED OR REJECTED, AND THE CONSEQUENCES

The FOS's award must require the complainant to notify the FOS before a specified date whether the determination is accepted or rejected. The FOS is required to notify the respondent of the outcome.[1]

This gives rise to three possibilities. The first, and simplest, is that the complainant rejects the determination. The FOS award will then be of no effect, and the complainant will generally be free to pursue whatever other remedies they wish.

The second is that the complainant fails to notify the FOS whether they accept or reject the determination. If this happens, under the compulsory jurisdiction the complainant is deemed to have rejected the award[2] unless the complainant later seeks to accept the determination and the FOS considers that the failure to reply was caused by 'exceptional circumstances'.[3] Although there is no explicit guidance on this rule, this will raise similar issues as those which arise when the FOS is considering whether there were exceptional circumstances which justify a departure from the time limits to bringing a complaint (see Chapter 6).

Slightly different rules apply to the voluntary jurisdiction. DISP 4.2.5R states that, provided the complainant accepts an award within the time specified for doing so, the determination will be binding on the VJ Participant. That means that, if the award is not accepted in time, it will not be binding.

---

1 FSMA, s.228. DISP 4.2.4R states that the FOS has the same powers to make determinations and awards under the voluntary jurisdiction as they have under the compulsory jurisdiction.

2 FSMA, s.228(6).

3 DISP 3.6.6R(4A).

The third possibility is that the determination is accepted by the complainant. Where this happens, the determination is binding on both the complainant and the respondent and is stated to be 'final'.[4] For the voluntary jurisdiction, a determination is simply said to be 'binding' on the VJ Participant, and enforceable in court, with no suggestion that it is binding on the complainant.[5]

The effect of acceptance

The authorities show that, once a FOS determination is accepted, the complaint is resolved once and for all. This will preclude a complainant from accepting an award for, say, £150,000, but then trying to commence court proceedings for any losses in excess of this.

That was the position in *Clark v In Focus Asset Management & Tax Solutions Ltd* [2014] EWCA Civ 118,[6] where the claimants had accepted an award under the compulsory jurisdiction, stated to be without prejudice to their right to bring further court proceedings. They commenced proceedings for the rest of their alleged losses. The Court of Appeal ruled that the award was binding and precluded legal proceedings in which the cause of action was constituted by the same facts as those on which the complaint was based. FOS decisions were sufficiently judicial so as to engage the principle of *res judicata.* They rejected the idea that, because the FOS's jurisdiction is there to aid consumers, it should be seen as additional to their right to also bring complaints before a court, even after a FOS determination had been accepted by them. Nor was it determinative that the FOS dealt with complaints rather than causes of action. That was because, for *res judicata* to occur, it was enough that the FOS decides a question posed by facts constituting a cause of action. As Arden LJ said at paragraph [77]:

4 FSMA, s.228(5).

5 DISP 4.2.5R.

6 See also *Andrews v SBJ Benefit Consultants Ltd* [2010] EWHC 2875 (Ch), which is to similar effect.

> '*it is sufficient that he decides whether the facts underlying a cause of action give rise to any claim as between the complainant and the adviser and whether the claimant has any remedy against the adviser relative to those facts. The fact that the remedy is not the same as would be awarded in a court of law is also not a requirement of res judicata…if the complainant were (unwisely) to accept an award offering him only an apology, res judicata would apply if he chose to bring court proceedings. His wiser course would be to reject the award altogether in those circumstances.*'

Arden LJ also gave guidance on how the court, when faced with a further action which had arguably already been determined by the FOS, should approach whether the second action was permissible. She said, at paragraph [79] that:

> '*the court would have to consider whether this was the same complaint and if so whether the ombudsman had determined the question raised by this complaint. The court would have to look at the detailed documentation.*'

In the Northern Irish decision of *Morton v First Trust Financial Services Ltd*. [2015] NIQB 46, Weatherup J declined to strike out a claim on the basis that a later court action was an abuse of process. He said that it would have required more than an analysis on the papers.

This means that not all later Court actions would be barred by the doctrine of *res judicata*, even if a determination had been accepted. According to Arden LJ, this will depend on the whether '*the substance of the proceedings asserted before the courts are the same as that before the Ombudsman Service*'.[7] It is, however, clear that an attempt to bring a Court claim so as to get round the monetary limits on FOS awards is impermissible.

The burden of showing that the facts constituting the cause of action relied on in the later Court proceedings formed the basis of the FOS complaint is on the defendant.[8]

---

7 *Clark v In Focus* at [89].

Clark was a case that concerned *res judicata* i.e. whether the cause of action had already been decided on. The Courts have long recognised that even though a claim may not strictly be subject to *res judicata*, it may nevertheless be an abuse of process because it is one which could and should have been brought in earlier proceedings. This is the so-called *Henderson v Henderson*[9] doctrine, where the Court will take a broad merits based view as to whether a second action is precluded by an earlier one, albeit that no issue estoppel has arisen. Whilst the Court of Appeal did not find it necessary to consider whether the *Henderson* rule would have applied on the facts of *Clark*, once it is recognised a FOS award may give rise to *res judicata*, this ought to mean that the *Henderson* doctrine can also apply. The Northern Irish Courts have reached the same conclusion (see the decision of Weartherup J. in *Morton*, discussed further above).

Second actions before the FOS

What happens where the complainant brings a second complaint before the FOS in respect of the same subject matter? Or where the complainant seeks to complain to the FOS after pursuing the same claim in litigation?

The first complaint will either have been dealt with by the FOS or the Court. Where the Court has previously considered it, the FOS has the power under to dismiss a complaint without considering the merits if it has already been decided by a Court or is presently subject to Court proceedings.[10]

Under these provisions, the dismissal by the FOS is not mandatory. Instead, the FOS 'may' decide to dismiss the claim. Where the matter has already been decided by Court proceedings, we consider that the facts should be highly exceptional before the FOS decides to hear the complaint. Indeed, in *Clark*, the FOS's submissions to the Court were

8 *Clark v In Focus* at [81].

9 (1843) 3 Hare 100.

10 See Chapter 8.

to the effect that they had no record of such a second complaint ever having been brought to them, and that their inclination would be to dismiss it.

Where the subject matter of the complaint has previously been considered by the FOS as opposed to a Court, it may also be dismissed, unless material new evidence which is likely to affect the outcome has subsequently become available to the complainant. This is obviously meant to be a hard threshold to overcome. Challenging a FOS decision that it will not hear a second complaint will be difficult.[11]

It is presently unclear whether the FOS would have jurisdiction to consider a second complaint in respect of a matter already determined and the FOS's decision accepted. That question was expressly left open in R *(Cook) v FOS* [2009] EWHC 426 (Admin).[12] We consider that the principle of finality and the fact that accepted decisions are 'binding' and 'final'[13] ought to mean that a second complaint is barred in these circumstances.

The FOS also publishes data about the number complaints against individual firms, and the number of complaints that are upheld against such firms.

11 See *R (Cook) v FOS* [2009] EWHC 426 (Admin), where Walker J. rejected a judicial review of the FOS's refusal to look into a decision again. It was thought significant both before the FOS and the Court that the claimants could have obtained the 'new' material with reasonable diligence earlier. A similar approach was taken in *R (Duff) v FOS* [2006] EWHC 1704 (Admin). See Chapters 9 and 16.

12 At [61].

13 FSMA, s. 228(5).

CHAPTER FIFTEEN ENFORCEMENT OF FOS AWARDS IN COURT

In Chapter 14 we looked at the circumstances under which a court will hear a claim that has already been determined by the FOS, where the FOS's award has been accepted by the complainant. In general, the Court will not allow the same complaint to be litigated again in Court.

This chapter considers a different situation: where the complainant has accepted a FOS decision, and seeks to enforce that award against the respondent.

Enforcement of a FOS award

Once the FOS has determined a complaint and this has been accepted, most respondents will comply and, if needs be, pay any sum found to be due. DISP 3.7.12R obliges respondents promptly to comply with awards, directions, or settlements.

In the event that this does not happen, FSMA contains a mechanism by which the FOS award can be enforced as if it were a Court judgment.[1]

By DISP 3.7.7R, the FOS will maintain a register of its awards. A monetary award, including interest, which has been so registered can be enforced as if it were an order of the County Court, should the County Court so order.[2] This means that permission must first be sought from the Court before enforcement can be sought. One way of doing that would be to issue a Part 8 Claim Form and make an application in those proceedings.

1 FSMA, s. 229(8) and Sch 17, para 16. DISP 4.2.5R provides that a binding award under the voluntary jurisdiction can be enforced in Court by the complainant.

2 FSMA, Sch 17, para 16.

Likewise, an order for directions can be enforced by way of an injunction.[3] In most cases, that can be done through commencing proceedings using a Part 8 Claim Form. As set out in Chapter 13, when granting directions, the FOS is not limited to what a Court could order.[4] But, as pointed out by Lewison J in *Bunney v Burns Anderson PLC*,[5] this gives rise to a conundrum. If the court could not grant an injunction to take the steps directed (for instance, an apology), then how can it do so under FSMA? Lewison J did not have to answer this question in *Bunney*.

One possibility is that FSMA grants the court the power to make an injunction when it would not otherwise be able to. In equity, there would be no power for a court to order an injunction for, say, an apology. But FSMA may be said to enable it to do so, if contained in a FOS direction.

Nevertheless, injunctions are discretionary. Because the consequences of a failure to comply with an injunction can be severe (namely, contempt of court), the court is not required to make an injunction in the terms of a FOS direction. It has a discretion. Thus, it may be that a judge would refuse to enforce a FOS award that was vague, impossible for the court to supervise, or where exposing the respondent to the possibility of contempt proceedings for non-compliance would be disproportionate.

Set-off against FOS awards

In view of DISP 3.7.12R, and the obligation on respondents to comply with FOS awards promptly, there is a question mark as to how far a respondent can exercise a right of set-off against a FOS award.

Where a monetary award is made in favour of a complainant, there seems to be no logical reason why the respondent could not set-off the

3 FSMA, s. 229(9).

4 DISP 3.7.11R.

5 [2007] EWHC 1240 (Ch) at [74].

amount of its liability. After all, the financial result to the complainant would be the same. Moreover, the obligation to comply promptly with a FOS award does not say in terms that a set-off is impermissible. This is especially so given that if the FOS award can be enforced as if they were a court judgment, and there are well-established rights of set-off against court judgments.

Limitation Periods

We are not aware of any cases that have tested the limitation period for enforcing a FOS award. It seems likely that the complainant would have six years to enforce their award, either under:

- Section 24 of the Limitation Act 1980, the time limit for enforcing judgments. This would be on the basis that, providing the court so orders, FOS awards are enforceable as if they were County Court judgments.
- Section 9 of the Limitation Act 1980, the time limit for actions to recover sums recoverable by statute.

It would then be arguable whether the starting point for limitation purposes is the date of the final decision, or the date that the complainant accepts the award.

CHAPTER SIXTEEN
INTERACTION BETWEEN THE FOS AND LITIGATION

In this chapter, we consider the ways in which FOS complaints interact with litigation in the courts, aside from the questions of *res judicata* and enforcement which are considered elsewhere, in Chapters 14 and 15.

Stay of proceedings where there is an extant FOS complaint

Normally, a complainant will refer their complaint to the FOS instead of litigation, or with litigation as a fall-back position if the FOS does not find in their favour.

However, it may be that a complainant has no choice but to commence court proceedings due to the imminent expiration of a limitation period,[1] but then wishes to commence proceedings before the FOS. Likewise, the FOS decision may be taking so long that the complainant is forced to issue court proceedings because of limitation concerns.

However, the FOS may dismiss a complaint without consideration of the merits where proceedings are under way, unless all the parties or the court has agreed to stay those proceeding so that the matter may be considered by the FOS.[2]

Accordingly, the two processes should not run concurrently: either the court proceedings are stayed to allow the FOS to consider the complaint, or the proceedings are not stayed and the FOS rejects the complaint.

In *Templars Estates Ltd v National Westminster Bank PLC*_[2016] EWHC 2020 (Comm), the claimant had issued proceedings to avoid the expiration of limitation, but then wished to pursue a FOS com-

---

1 Not that it ought to be in doubt, but commencing FOS proceedings will not stop limitation from running: *Clarke v Argyle Consulting Ltd* 2011 SLT 180.

2 DISP 3.3.4A R and 3.3.4B G.

plaint. The defendants submitted that the claimants were trying to have their cake and eat it: even if they won before the FOS, there was no guarantee that they would accept the offer and bring an end to the proceedings. In fact, the claimant undertook that they would accept any award made by the FOS, and not come back to court if they won before it. On that basis a stay was granted.

Referral by the FOS to another complaints scheme or the court

DISP 3.4 sets out provisions pursuant to which the FOS may refer complaints to other complaint schemes or the court. For the former, the test set out in DISP 3.4.1R is that the FOS may so refer where it considers the other scheme to be more suitable, and the complainant consents to the referral. For the latter, the FOS has a power, with the complainant's consent, to refer a complaint to court to consider it as a test case.

The FOS's power to dismiss a complaint so that it can be heard by a court as a test case is set out in DISP 3.4.2R. The preconditions to the FOS referring a test case to court are reasonably complex, but they may be broken down as follows:

1. Before the FOS has made any determination, the respondent may request a referral, on the basis that the complaint raises '*an important or novel point of law with significant consequences*'.[3] Evidently, this is quite narrow in scope. It is likely to cover situations where there is a market wide issue.

2. The respondent must provide an undertaking in favour of the complainant that if the complainant or the respondent commences court proceedings in any UK court within six months of the FOS dismissing the claim, the respondent will pay the complainant's reasonable costs of the proceedings.[4]

3 DISP 3.4.2R (1)(a).

4 DISP 3.4.2R (1)(b).

3. Finally, the FOS must conclude that the complaint raises an important or novel point of law with important consequences, which is more suitable for determination by the court as a test case.[5] Factors that the FOS will take into account when making that decision include whether the point of law is central to the dispute, how important it is, the significance to the respondent, the amount at stake, and the remedies that a court could impose.[6]

The admissibility of FOS awards in court proceedings

It may be that a party wishes to rely on a particular finding made by the FOS in subsequent litigation.

It is a rule of evidence in English courts that a decision in one set of court proceedings is not admissible in later court proceedings to prove the facts that were found by judge in the first set of proceedings. Instead, the same facts must be proven again before the second judge.[7] This is the so-called rule in *Hollington v Hewthorn*. The rule has undergone considerable criticism and is kept within narrow bounds. For instance, it was not applied where there was a report by the Department of Transport's Air Accident Investigation Branch about an aeroplane accident: the report was admitted in a later civil claim about that accident and was not barred from admission by the *Hollington* rule. The report was from a body with particular expertise, which the court did not itself have, and this supported the idea that it should be taken into account.[8]

There remains a debate about whether FOS awards are admissible or not in subsequent proceedings as evidence of the facts or conclusions contained within them. On the one hand, the FOS is a tribunal for at

5 DISP 3.4.2R (2).

6 DISP 3.4.3G.

7 *Hollington v F Hewthorn* [1943] KB 587.

8 *Rogers v Hoyle* [2015] QB 265, containing the first instance and appellate decisions.

least some purposes,[9] and reaches conclusions based on the evidence before it, which would suggest that its findings should not be admissible. On the other hand, the courts regularly defer to the expertise of the FOS in financial services. As far as we are aware, there has been no judicial determination of this question.

9 *R (Calland) v FOS* [2013] EWHC 1327 (Admin) at [35].

CHAPTER SEVENTEEN CHALLENGING FOS DECISIONS IN THE COURTS: JUDICIAL REVIEW AND OTHER OPTIONS

A party that dislikes a FOS award has limited options. There is no appeal process within the FOS rules, and if the complainant accepts the award, it becomes final and binding on the respondent.[1] The respondent is obliged to comply with a final decision that the complainant has accepted.[2] Indeed, a persistent failure to comply with a FOS award may lead to regulatory action by the FCA, potentially even leading to a loss of authorisation.[3]

This chapter sets out the options that exist to challenge FOS awards:

1. The usual method of challenging a FOS award is to seek a judicial review of the decision. The main focus of this chapter is to set out the bases on which judicial review has been sought, and the areas where a review is most likely to be successful.

2. Occasionally, a respondent might seek to challenge an award by waiting for the complainant's claim to enforce the award. In some circumstances, the respondent might be able to defeat the claim by pointing to defects in the FOS award itself, such as an absence of jurisdiction.

In general, the courts have been resistant to challenges to FOS awards. Many firms have tried, and only a few have succeeded. The reasons for this are contained within the legislation itself. The FOS was expressly set up to resolve disputes quickly and with minimum formality, based on what the FOS views as fair and reasonable.[4] From the very earliest

---

1 FSMA, s. 228(5). See further Chapter 14.

2 DISP 3.7.12R.

3 For example, see the Final Notices for Glyn Goodyear dated 14 April 2016 and for Foreman Financial Services Limited dated 23 October 2017.

judicial review cases the courts have warned against '*over-active judicial intervention*' and are '*very wary*' of overturning FOS decisions.[5]

On the other hand, the courts are more ready to intervene where the FOS has over-reached its jurisdiction.[6]

Unhappy complainants have also gone to court to argue that the FOS was wrong. Here, it is very difficult to succeed. One reason for this is that complainants have other options available to them: a negative result is not binding on the complainant and they are free to pursue fresh claims against the respondent.

Procedure

This is not a book on judicial review procedure, and anybody that is considering such action should consult specialist texts. Nevertheless, there are some basic elements of procedure which any challenging party should be aware of.

Of particular importance in judicial review claims is CPR 54.5(1): '*The claim form must be filed—(a) promptly; and (b) in any event not later than 3 months after the grounds to make the claim first arose.*'

Both elements of the rule are important: judicial review claims have been refused even though they were issued within 3 months of the relevant decision because the court concluded that they were not prompt.

In addition, the applicant is expected to comply with the pre-action protocol for judicial review, by sending a letter before claim and giving the defendant 14 days to respond. It is important to note that complying with the pre-action protocol will not extend time for filing the claim form, though it is relevant to the promptness of the claim.

4 FSMA, s. 225(1), s. 228(2) and s. 229(2).

5 *R (Norwich and Peterborough Building Society) v FOS* [2002] EWHC 2379 (Admin) at [77-78].

6 *R (Bluefin Insurance Services Ltd) v FOS* [2014] EWHC 3413 (Admin)

In any case challenging a FOS award, the defendant will be the FOS itself. It will also be appropriate to name the other party to the FOS award as an 'interested party'.[7] So, a firm who was a respondent to FOS action and who is challenging an award should name the complainant as an interested party; a complainant that is challenging an award should name the firm that was the respondent before the FOS proceedings as an interested party.

Depending on the circumstances, it may also be appropriate to include the FCA as an interested party: this may be appropriate where the FOS decision is said to impinge on or relate to processes instigated by the FCA.[8]

The Claim Form should comply with Part 8 of the CPR, meaning that it should be accompanied by any written evidence that the claimant wishes to rely upon.[9] It must then be served within 7 days after the date of issue.[10]

The defendant (i.e. the FOS) and the interested party then have 21 days to file an Acknowledgement of Service,[11] which should include a summary of grounds for contesting the claim. A failure to file an Acknowledgement of Service does not mean that the judicial review will automatically succeed, though a party that fails to file an Acknowledgement will be unable to take part in a hearing as to whether permission for the judicial review should be granted.[12]

---

7 Provision is made for the inclusion of Interested Parties in CPR 54.6(1). There are no specific rules referable to reviews of FOS decisions, but CPR 54APD para 5.1 refers to judicial reviews of courts and tribunals, and states that the parties to the decision should be named as interested parties.

8 As occurred in *R (Full Circle Asset Management Ltd) v FOS* [2017] EWHC 323 (Admin), which raised issues concerning a skilled person's report accepted by the FCA, and in *R (Mazarona Properties Ltd) v FOS* [2017] EWHC 1135 (Admin), relating to a review of interest rate hedging products instigated by the FCA.

9 CPR 8.5.

10 CPR 54.7.

11 CPR 54.8.

12 CPR 54.9.

The court will then proceed to consider whether permission should be granted for judicial review to proceed. Permission depends on the court being satisfied that there is an arguable case for the claim. Normally, the court will reach this conclusion on the papers (i.e. without a hearing). If permission is not given, the claimant can then request an oral hearing to reconsider the matter. There will be such a hearing unless the court concludes that the application is totally without merit.[13]

If the court does give permission for the judicial review, then the defendant (i.e. the FOS) and the interested party may file a detailed Response to the claim, together with any evidence that they wish to rely upon, within 35 days of the order giving permission.[14]

The judicial review will then proceed to a substantive hearing, which is usually conducted using written evidence. It is unusual to have cross-examination of witnesses in a judicial review claim.

Grounds of challenge

The categories of challenge considered below are not unique to judicial reviews of FOS decisions. They depend on the general principles of judicial review, which are applicable to all bodies whose conduct can be challenged through that process. That being said, we set out below how those principles tend to apply in the context of judicial reviews of the FOS.

It is important to note that none of the grounds for review is that the FOS simply 'got it wrong'. The courts will not engage with that question, unless it can be shown that the wrongness of the decision falls into one of the following categories.

No jurisdiction

If the FOS did not have jurisdiction to reach the decision that it did, then the court will quash the decision.

---

13 CPR 54.12(7).

14 CPR 54.14.

There is a particular issue with the 3 month time limit for judicial review actions when challenging jurisdiction. This is because the FOS will often resolve the question of its own jurisdiction at an early stage of proceedings (see Chapter 8). If the FOS rules that it does not have jurisdiction, then the complainant will obviously need to commence judicial review proceedings promptly. For a respondent to FOS proceedings that is challenging jurisdiction, however, should it issue a Claim Form immediately, or only after the final decision on the complaint?

The FOS tends to argue that there is no need to challenge jurisdiction until the final decision has been reached, because it will continue to review its own jurisdiction until the final decision on the merits.[15] The courts have, however, considered judicial review claims prior to the final decision.[16] But the FOS's general position means that respondent firms may be able to choose between the earlier date and the later date for a judicial review. If a respondent decides to await the final decision on the merits, it should send a letter to the FOS soon after its (initial) decision on jurisdiction so as to obtain explicit agreement from the FOS that jurisdiction will remain under review and that there is no need to issue a judicial review until after the final decision.

As to the substance of judicial review claims on jurisdiction, it will be necessary to show that the FOS has stepped outside the limits of its jurisdiction as set out under FSMA or DISP, or alternatively has refused to consider a complaint that it did have jurisdiction over. For details on the FOS's jurisdiction, see Chapter 3.

Generally, the courts appear to be more amenable to judicial review claims that relate to jurisdiction disputes than on other grounds. This is because the question of jurisdiction is not a question of what is 'fair and reasonable' but a question of law depending on statutory construction. If the FOS has misdirected itself on the law, either as to the legal test or the application of that test, then the court will review the FOS's conclusions. Nevertheless, in doing so, the court will usually apply the law to

---

15 *R (Chancery (UK) LLP) v FOS* [2015] EWHC 407 (Admin) at [78].

16 *R (Brinsons) v FOS* [2007] EWHC 2534 (Admin) at [29]; *R (Chancery (UK) Ltd) v FOS* [2015] EWHC 407 (Admin) at [80].

the facts as found by the FOS[17] and, despite the court's willingness to engage with arguments on jurisdiction, the vast majority of attempted judicial reviews on this basis have still failed.

The issue has been raised in the following cases:

1. In *R (Ropaigealach) v FOS* [2005] EWCA Civ 269, it was argued by a complainant that, amongst other things, the FOS had misapplied its own time limits, such that it did have jurisdiction to consider the complaint. The court rejected this argument, as the complaint was clearly out of time.

2. In *R (London Capital Group) v FOS* [2013] EWHC 2425 (Admin), the court considered whether the FOS has jurisdiction in relation to foreign exchange trading accounts. This involved a dispute as to whether such accounts involve investments specified in the RAO. The court concluded that the relevant accounts involved contracts for difference, and were therefore within the FOS's jurisdiction. The judicial review therefore failed.

3. In *R (Bluefin Insurance Services Ltd) v FOS* [2014] EWHC 3413 (Admin), the court considered whether a complainant was an eligible complainant (see Chapter 3). This was said to require a hard-edged finding of an objective fact, which the court was required to assess.[18] The court concluded that a director of a business, complaining about the administration of an insurance policy which he claimed should have protected him, was not a consumer. This was because the claim related to his acts as director, forming part of his business or trade.[19] Accordingly, the FOS did not have jurisdiction and the judicial review succeeded.

---

17 *R (Chancery (UK) LLP) v FOS* [2015] EWHC 407 (Admin) at [66-71].

18 At [67].

19 At [116-123].

4. In *R (Chancery (UK) LLP) v FOS* [2015] EWHC 407 (Admin), the question was whether tax advice involving collective investment schemes fell within the FOS's jurisdiction. The court concluded that tax advice and investment advice were not mutually exclusive: where there was advice on the merits of investments that fell within FSMA, the FOS had jurisdiction.[20]

5. In *R (Mazarona Properties Ltd) v FOS* [2017] EWHC 1135 (Admin), the court decided that the FOS had no jurisdiction to consider complaints arising out of a review of interest rate hedging products, instituted pursuant to an agreement with the FCA. The conduct of such a review is not a 'financial service' for the purpose of the FOS's jurisdiction.

Irrationality/Failure to take relevant factors into account

As we have noted above, a judicial review will not succeed because the FOS merely 'got it wrong' (unless, of course, the mistake goes to the FOS's jurisdiction). Instead, it will be necessary to show that the decision was so wrong that it was irrational. The test is whether the decision was '*so outrageous in its defiance of logic or of accepted moral standards that no sensible person who had applied his mind to the question to be decided could have arrived at it.*'[21]

In this context, the courts have distinguished between findings which rely upon the expertise of the decision maker, and findings where no expertise is needed. It is harder to challenge the former.[22] Nevertheless, it is not enough to argue that the FOS may have got findings of fact wrong: the test is still whether the finding of fact was irrational.

20 At [93-94].

21 *CSSU v Minister of the Civil Service* [1985] AC 374, quoted in *R (Aviva Life and Pensions (UK) Ltd) v FOS* [2017] EWHC 352 (Admin) at [58].

22 *R (Green) v FOS* [2012] EWHC 1253 (Admin) at [11].

Cases in which irrationality has been pursued as a ground for judicial review include:

1. In *R (IFG Financial Services Ltd) v FOS* [2005] EWHC 1153 (Admin), Stanley Burton J noted that the FOS is not bound to apply the law, and the FOS's view of what is fair and reasonable can only be challenged if the view is perverse or irrational.[23] Accordingly, the fact that the FOS did not apply the rule in *SAAMCO*[24] to the facts of the case did not mean that it was irrational. The reasons for the FOS's departure from the strict legal position were sufficiently clear.

2. *R (Garrison Investment Analysis) v FOS* [2006] EWHC 2466 (Admin) is a rare instance where an irrationality argument has succeeded. The challenge was limited to the calculation of quantum. The FOS had accepted that the complainants would have accepted some risk, yet his award proceeded on the basis that they would have accepted none. Sullivan J concluded that this was 'inexplicable' and quashed the decision on this point, indicating the approach that he considered the FOS should take when reconsidering the decision.

3. *R (Green) v FOS* [2012] EWHC 1253 (Admin) was a case in which an IFA argued that the FOS had been wrong to conclude that bad advice had been provided, and that the complainants would have acted differently if other advice had been given. The court noted the risk that the complainant's evidence was unreliable, but concluded that the FOS's decision was not irrational. This decision is notable, because the court implied that it would have reached a different conclusion if making the decision itself, but upheld the FOS's decision as rational.

4. In *R (Bankole) v FOS* [2012] EWHC 3555 (Admin) the complainant challenged the FOS's conclusion that he had received the respondent firm's final letter of response, triggering the 6

23 At [13].

24 *South Australia Asset Management Corp v York Montague* [1997] AC 191.

month period in which to pursue a complaint (see Chapter 3). The FOS had provided reasons for its conclusions and could not be overturned as irrational or unsupported by evidence.

5. *R (Walker) v FOS* [2013] NIQB 12 involved arguments that the FOS incorrectly reached conclusions as to the appropriateness of a mortgage. On the facts of the case, where the relevant matters had previously been considered by a court with the same outcome as the FOS, it is not surprising that the court held that the FOS's conclusions were reasonable.

6. In *R (Chancery (UK) LLP) v FOS* [2015] EWHC 407 (Admin), it was argued that the FOS was irrational not to dismiss the complaint as more suitable for determination by a court (see Chapter 16) on the basis that there were a large number of claims with similar issues, involving large sums of money. It was argued that the FOS was an inappropriate forum, but again the court concluded that the FOS was not irrational in concluding otherwise.

A different way of pursuing the same argument may be to say that the FOS failed to take into account a relevant consideration, or took into account an irrelevant consideration, such that the whole decision can be impeached.

In *R (Norwich and Peterborough Building Society) v FOS* [2002] EWHC 2379 (Admin) the court considered the FOS's approach to the Banking Code, stating that if the FOS misconstrued the Code then it failed to take into account a material consideration, such that its decision would be irrational.[25] On the other hand, if the Code was construed properly then the FOS would be given wide leeway in its application of the Code. On the facts of the case, the FOS was found to have misconstrued the Code, but the judicial review failed on the basis that the FOS's decision was supportable for other reasons.

25 At [79].

Procedural fairness

There are a number of grounds on which FOS decisions might be challenged by reference to procedural fairness.

Although a concept with a long history, many such challenges would now be pursued by reference to Article 6 of the European Convention on Human Rights. Article 6 states that every person to a dispute is entitled to a fair and public hearing within a reasonable time, conducted by an independent and impartial tribunal.

The FOS is a tribunal for the purpose of Article 6,[26] and clearly it must act fairly in reaching its decisions.[27] However, the nature of the FOS as a decision-making body means that it is not bound to take the same approach as a court would. For example, a court would not normally consider matters beyond those put forward by the parties. The FOS, on the other hand, is entitled to do so as long as the parties have an opportunity to address those matters. This is in part a reflection of the fact that the parties, and complainants in particular, are not usually represented.

Likewise, an element of the right to a fair hearing is the requirement that a party ought to know the allegations pursued against it. In *R (Bruce) v FOS* [2007] Pens LR 287, a partner in a respondent firm argued that she had not been notified of the complaint prior to the FOS's provisional decision. In consequence, she argued, she had not been able to participate in the investigation of the facts and there had been a breach of natural justice. The court disagreed. First, the firm was on notice as to the complaint even if an individual partner was not.[28] Secondly, the partner failed to put forward any defence to the claim even during the judicial review. Hodge J refused to remit the decision to the FOS where there was no reason for thinking that a different decision would be reached.

---

26 *R (Calland) v FOS* [2013] EWHC 1327 (Admin) at [35].

27 *R (Green) v FOS* [2003] EWHC 338 (Admin) at [39].

28 This is now dealt with explicitly by DISP 3.1.3R.

It is also important to note that the procedures adopted by the FOS (through adjudicators, and the use of provisional decisions) will usually mean that by the time the final decision is made, the basis of the complainant is obvious to the respondent.[29] This means that the scope for challenging a FOS decision on the basis that the respondent did not know the case they had to meet is highly limited.

It is possible that severe delay by the FOS might constitute a contravention of Article 6 of the European Convention on Human Rights, which refers to decisions being reached within a reasonable time. We are only aware of one case in which this argument was pursued: *R (Calland) v FOS* [2013] EWHC 1327 (Admin). The final decision in that case had taken six years, but the court found that this was largely caused by the attitude of the firm, and that in any event it would not lead to the reversal of the decision absent some unfairness cause by the delay.

In short, there are great difficulties with judicially reviewing the FOS based on grounds of procedural unfairness. However, we are of the view that the court would intervene if a procedure adopted by the FOS was palpably unfair. For example, if a FOS decision relied on key documents, or a witness statement, supplied by one party but not shown to the other party, the court might take a dim view of that approach.

Bias

There can be no doubt that a FOS decision would be reviewable if there was evidence that the decision was tainted by actual or apparent bias of an ombudsman. There is a long common law history to judicial reviews based on bias, but the case law will now also take into account Article 6 of the European Convention on Human Rights.

In order to show actual bias it would be necessary to show that the ombudsman deciding the complaint had a direct personal interest or connection to the matter, or something similar.

---

29 *R (Green) v FOS* [2003] EWHC 338 (Admin) at [42-52]

Given the difficulties in proving actual bias, it is more usual to argue that there were facts about the decision maker which give rise to apparent bias. The test for apparent bias is that the circumstances would lead a fair-minded and informed observer to conclude that there was a real possibility that the decision maker was biased.[30] In cases involving the judiciary, the way in which the judge conducts themselves both inside[31] and outside court[32] may give rise to apparent bias.

Accordingly, there might well be good grounds for challenge if it could be shown that the ombudsman, or possibly the adjudicator, had a close personal or professional relationship with either the complainant or the respondent firm. Likewise, any particular animosity shown by the ombudsman or adjudicator could give rise to apparent bias.

No reported case has featured such facts. It was argued in both *R (Bamber) v FOS* [2009] EWCA Civ 593 and *R (Heather Moor & Edgecomb) v FOS* [2009] EWHC 2701 (Admin) that the relationship between the FOS and the FCA (the FSA, as it then was) demonstrated that the FOS was not independent, but that argument was rejected.[33]

Likewise, *R (Calland) v FOS* [2013] EWHC 1327 (Admin) featured allegations of 'collusion' between the FOS and the FCA (then FSA), but which the court dismissed.[34] The court considered that it was a 'somewhat tangled' way for complaints to arise, but held there had been nothing improper in the FCA referring customer complaints to the FOS.[35]

30 *Porter v Magill* [2001] UKHL 67; [2002] 2 AC 357 at [102-103].

31 For example, if a judge is openly antagonistic towards a party: *Howell v Millais* [2007] EWCA Civ 720.

32 E.g. in *Locabail v Bayfield Properties* [2000] 2 WLR 870 at [89], a judge's articles in various publications, antagonistic to insurers, was found to give rise to apparent bias.

33 At [16-19].

34 See [25].

35 See [21], [55]. [57] and [120].

Insufficiency of reasons

A FOS decision should set out sufficient reasons that the parties (and the court) can understand the facts and reasoning which the led the FOS to its result.[36]

However, the requirement is not as high as it would be for a court. Given the informal nature of FOS complaints, it will be sufficient if the FOS approaches matters on a common sense basis, and it is not required to address every argument put forward by the parties, as long as the conclusion is clear.[37]

This is an area where the courts have been known to find fault with the FOS and, on at least one occasion, remit the decision to the FOS:

1. In *R (Duff) v FOS* [2006] EWHC 1704 at [6] the court concluded that there had 'perhaps' been insufficient reasons given by the FOS on a particular point, but agreed with the FOS that the complainant should be left to his alternative remedy of commencing litigation (see below).

2. In *R (Garrison Investment Analysis) v FOS* [2006] EWHC 2466 (Admin), the FOS's approach to quantum calculations was found to be 'inexplicable',[38] and the case was remitted to the FOS. This finding was supported by a conclusion that the FOS's approach had been irrational (see above).

Moreover, there have been cases in which the FOS itself accepted that its decision included insufficient explanation, and agreed to reconsider matters without the matter proceeding to judicial review.[39]

---

36 *R (Young Ridgway) v FOS* [2004] EWHC 3371 (Admin) at [30-33].

37 *R (Garrison Investment Analysis) v FOS* [2006] EWHC 2466 (Admin) at [5].

38 At [21].

39 *R (Full Circle Asset Management) v FOS* [2017] EWHC 323 (Admin); *R (Aviva Life and Pensions (UK) Ltd) v FOS* [2017] EWHC 352 (Admin); *Berkeley Burke Sipp Administration v Charlton* [2017] EWHC 2396 (Comm).

Any party challenging a FOS decision on the basis that insufficient reasons were given should remember that the first decision may be overturned, but the FOS will be given an opportunity to reconsider. The FOS may well reach the same conclusion the second time, albeit with fuller reasoning.

Lack of an oral hearing

In Chapter 10, we set out the FOS's approach to oral hearings, and the fact that they are very much the exception rather than the rule. This is despite the fact that the lack of an oral hearing is an argument that has often been pursued in judicial review proceedings as a ground for challenging decisions, and the courts have indicated that in appropriate cases an oral hearing might be necessary:

1. In *R (Ropaigealach) v FOS* [2005] EWCA Civ 269, the court stated that there is no entitlement to an oral hearing where the decision-maker is of the view that they have sufficient information.[40] This would suggest that the decision not to hold an oral hearing could only be challenged if the decision-maker irrationally thought that one was unnecessary.

2. In *R (Heather Moor & Edgecomb) v FOS* [2008] EWCA Civ 642, the Court of Appeal gave a more fully reasoned decision, suggesting that if the determination of a complaint involved the resolution of disputes as to what was said at a meeting, then fairness would require an oral hearing.[41] However, it was also suggested that it is not normally necessary for such a hearing, and that the Article 6 right to a public hearing is satisfied by the availability of judicial review proceedings.[42]

3. *R (Heather Moor & Edgecomb) v FOS* [2009] EWHC 2701 (Admin) was a separate judicial review proceeding by the same firm (in relation to a different complaint). HHJ Davis stated

40 At [16].

41 At [58].

42 At [67].

that there may be cases in which a public hearing is necessary, but not where there is a comprehensive written record.[43]

4. In *R (Calland) v FOS* [2013] EWHC 1327 (Admin), Males J stated that he considered that it was up to the court – not the FOS – to decide whether fairness requires an oral hearing.[44] This suggests that irrationality is not the test, but again on the facts of the case before him Males J concluded that an oral hearing would have been unlikely to have assisted the FOS and so it was not necessary.

Arbitrariness, or not treating like cases alike

In *R (Heather Moor & Edgecomb) v FOS* [2008] EWCA Civ 642, the Court of Appeal noted another aspect of Convention rights, that FOS decisions could be challenged if they were demonstrably arbitrary: '*Arbitrariness on the part of the ombudsman, including an unreasoned and unjustified failure to treat like cases alike would be a ground for judicial review*'.[45]

However, the court noted the FOS's stated aim of consistency and dismissed the argument. In practice, it will be difficult to persuade a court that the FOS has acted in an arbitrary way, unless perhaps a FOS decision runs counter to the FOS's stated position on a particular issue.

Excessive use of an ombudsman's own knowledge

In judicial proceedings, there are limits on a judge's ability to rely on his/her own knowledge of facts that have not been presented to the court. 'Judicial notice' allows a judge to rely on matters that are common knowledge, but what is the position with the FOS? On the one hand, the FOS is established as a specialist scheme employing ombudsmen with knowledge of the industry. On the other hand, there

---

43 At [10].

44 At [79].

45 At [49].

is a danger of personal bias creeping in if the ombudsman relies on his/her own experience.

R (Williams) v FOS [2008] EWHC 2142 (Admin) suggests that there should be some limit on the use of personal experience, where complaints relate to rare or complicated historical matters.

At the same time, the case also shows the difficulties with judicially reviewing such a decision: it will be necessary to show that the FOS acted irrationally, a difficult test to satisfy.

Relevance of alternative remedies

There are conflicting decisions as to whether judicial review should be refused on the basis that the complainant has an 'alternative remedy'.

In *R (Duff) v FOS* [2006] EWHC 1704 (Admin) it was suggested that a successful judicial review in favour of a complainant would be 'very rare', on the basis that the complainant would always have the alternative remedy of court proceedings.[46] In general, judicial review will be refused when such alternative remedies exist.

On the other hand, *R (Walker) v FOS* [2013] NIQB 12 reached the opposite conclusion, noting that this approach would force the complainant into court proceedings, which the FOS was set up to avoid. This is a Northern Ireland case, but it would appear that a similar conclusion was reached by the English court in *R (Fisher) v FOS* (2014, unreported), which is to the effect that judicial review should not be refused because of the existence of alternative remedies.

The remedy in judicial review proceedings

If the judicial review is successful, then the appropriate order will depend on the grounds of the judicial review.

46 At [7].

If the FOS has no jurisdiction to consider the compliant, then the FOS's decision will be quashed and that will normally be the end of the FOS complaint.

If the FOS decision suffered from a procedural irregularity or insufficient reasons, then the usual order would be to quash the FOS's decision and to remit the complaint to the FOS to reconsider.

If the question is one of irrationality, then the usual order would be to quash the FOS's decision and remit it for reconsideration, unless there would only be one rational answer. If there is only one rational answer, then the FOS can be directed to reach that answer.[47]

The court has a jurisdiction to quash the decision as a whole, or just one part of it: in *R (Aviva Life & Pensions (UK) Ltd) v FOS* [2017] EWHC 352 (Admin), a decision was quashed because of inadequate reasons. The firm suggested that the FOS should only reconsider the element of the complaint that the FOS had upheld. On the facts of that case, the entirety of the decision was quashed.

Costs of the judicial review

In general, the costs of a judicial review of the FOS will follow the normal principles in such cases: the victor would expect to receive their costs from the losing party.

However, special factors may apply to a judicial review, which may give rise to more unusual cost orders: if the judicial review is pursued by a firm who was a respondent to the FOS proceedings, it is possible that the court may make an order that the firm pay the complainant's costs, irrespective of the outcome. There is only one reported case in which this has happened, where the dispute revolved around the quantum of

47 *R (Aviva Life and Pensions (UK) Ltd) v FOS* [2017] EWHC 352 (Admin) at [57]. Also see *R (Garrison Investment Analysis) v FOS* [2006] EWHC 2466 (Admin), where the Court concluded that the FOS had taken the wrong approach to its calculation of loss, by reference to the Bank of England Base Rate. Concluding that the complainants would have invested in equities, the Court commented that the losses should have been calculated by reference to an appropriate index.

compensation rather than the validity of the complaint.[48] It is notable that, in that case, the order was made by a judge at first instance, and Laws LJ in the Court of Appeal suggested that he might not have made the same order.

Generally speaking, the FOS will be awarded its costs if it successfully sees off a judicial review. An interested party will not be awarded costs unless it can show that it had a sufficiently good reason for attending in addition to the FOS.[49] In one case, an attempt by a bank, as an interested party, to obtain its costs was given very short shrift.[50]

Refusing to comply with the decision

The majority of this chapter has focussed on judicial review, and there is no doubt that a judicial review against the FOS is the conventional way to challenge a FOS award.

However, the case of *Bunney v Burns Anderson* [2007] EWHC 1240 (Ch) suggests another avenue that may be available to firms who are respondents to FOS complaints: to refuse to comply with the award and await enforcement action from the complainant. The judge in that case suggested that firms could resist enforcement without starting a judicial review, at least where the challenge was to the validity of the FOS award, not its merits.[51]

So, if a respondent firm wishes to argue that the FOS exceeded its jurisdiction, then it could leave it to the complainant to start court action. This would require the complainant to pay the court fees and expose the complainant to legal costs. It would also avoid the three month time period applicable to judicial review claims.

---

48 *R (Towry Law Financial Services Ltd) v FOS* [2004] EWCA Civ 1701.

49 *Bolton Metropolitan District Council v Secretary of State for the Environment* [1995] 1 WLR 1176

50 *R (Mazarona Properties Ltd) v FOS* [2017] EWHC 1135 (Admin).

51 At paragraphs [50 – 52].

There are some health warnings to such an approach, though:

1. The FCA might not look kindly on a respondent taking this approach. As noted in the opening paragraph of this chapter, firms have had their authorisation cancelled for failing to comply with FOS decisions. The context of the *Bunney* decision is important in this regard: the firm in that case was willing to comply with the FOS decision up to the financial cap. It was only refusing to comply with the FOS decision to the extent that it was more costly than the cap.

2. The judge in *Bunney v Burns Anderson* recognised that his conclusions might be controversial, and stated he would be receptive to an application for permission to appeal.[52] A future judge, or the Court of Appeal, might disagree with his conclusions.

Appeals under the Arbitration Act 1996 are not available

Finally, there is a mode of challenging a FOS decision which has been resoundingly rejected. In *Berkeley Burke Sipp Administration v Charlton* [2017] EWHC 2396 (Comm), it was argued that a FOS decision could be challenged under section 69 of the Arbitration Act 1996. Teare J concluded that the FOS's jurisdiction is not derived from an agreement between the parties, and as such is not a form of arbitration.

52 At [79].

CHAPTER EIGHTEEN
THE RESPONDENT'S INSOLVENCY: THE FSCS AND THE INSURANCE ACTS

What does the complainant do if they have obtained a monetary award from the FOS, but the respondent firm does not have any money to pay?

Where the respondent is insolvent,[1] a 'protected claimant' can make a claim against the Financial Services Compensation Scheme, which is a creation of Part XV of FSMA.

Most financial services firms will also have indemnity insurance. It may be that some of these policies exclude sums that have been ordered to be paid by the FOS (or other ombudsman). But, for those that do not, the liability embodied by a FOS award may be capable of enforcement against the respondent's insurer.

For liabilities incurred after 1 August 2015, this question will be governed by the Third Parties (Rights against Insurers) Act 2010. Essentially, that Act provides that if a relevant person (here, the insolvent respondent) incurs a liability to a third party, that liability can once established be enforced directly against the insurer. A liability can be established either through using the procedure set out in s.2 of the Act (which will generally be the case for FOS awards), obtaining a judgment or decree, or through an enforceable agreement (which will be the case where FOS proceedings have resulted in a settlement agreement).[2]

For liabilities incurred before 1 August 2015, the provisions of the more complex Third Parties (Rights against Insurers) Act 1930 will apply. Put simply, by s.1 of that Act, where a respondent undergoes one of the insolvency events specified in s.1(1)(a) or (b), and any liability has been

1 COMP 6.3.1R defines various situations in which a firm is in default.

2 Section 1(4) of the 2010 Act.

incurred by the insured, the rights against the insurer will pass to the third party complainant.

MORE BOOKS BY LAW BRIEF PUBLISHING

A selection of our other titles available now:

'A Practical Guide to the 2018 Jackson Personal Injury and Costs Reforms' by Andrew Mckie
'A Guide to Consent in Clinical Negligence Post-Montgomery' by Lauren Sutherland QC
'A Practical Guide to Running Housing Disrepair and Cavity Wall Claims: 2nd Edition' by Andrew Mckie & Ian Skeate
'A Practical Guide to the General Data Protection Regulation (GDPR)' by Keith Markham
'A Practical Guide to Digital and Social Media Law for Lawyers' by Sherree Westell
'A Practical Guide to Holiday Sickness Claims, 2nd Edition' by Andrew Mckie & Ian Skeate
'A Practical Guide to Inheritance Act Claims by Adult Children Post-Ilott v Blue Cross' by Sheila Hamilton Macdonald
'A Practical Guide to Elderly Law' by Justin Patten
'Arguments and Tactics for Personal Injury and Clinical Negligence Claims' by Dorian Williams
'A Practical Guide to QOCS and Fundamental Dishonesty' by James Bentley
'A Practical Guide to Drone Law' by Rufus Ballaster, Andrew Firman, Eleanor Clot
'Practical Mediation: A Guide for Mediators, Advocates, Advisers, Lawyers, and Students in Civil, Commercial, Business, Property, Workplace, and Employment Cases' by Jonathan Dingle with John Sephton
'Practical Horse Law: A Guide for Owners and Riders' by Brenda Gilligan
'A Comparative Guide to Standard Form Construction and Engineering Contracts' by Jon Close
'A Practical Guide to Compliance for Personal Injury Firms Working With Claims Management Companies' by Paul Bennett
'A Practical Guide to the Landlord and Tenant Act 1954: Commercial Tenancies'

by Richard Hayes & David Sawtell
'A Practical Guide to Personal Injury Claims Involving Animals' by Jonathan Hand
'A Practical Guide to Psychiatric Claims in Personal Injury' by Liam Ryan
'Introduction to the Law of Community Care in England and Wales' by Alan Robinson
'A Practical Guide to Dog Law for Owners and Others' by Andrea Pitt
'Ellis and Kevan on Credit Hire, 5th Edition' by Aidan Ellis & Tim Kevan
'RTA Allegations of Fraud in a Post-Jackson Era: The Handbook, 2nd Edition' by Andrew Mckie
'RTA Personal Injury Claims: A Practical Guide Post-Jackson' by Andrew Mckie
'On Experts: CPR35 for Lawyers and Experts' by David Boyle
'An Introduction to Personal Injury Law' by David Boyle
'A Practical Guide to Claims Arising From Accidents Abroad and Travel Claims' by Andrew Mckie & Ian Skeate
'A Practical Guide to Cosmetic Surgery Claims' by Dr Victoria Handley
'A Practical Guide to Chronic Pain Claims' by Pankaj Madan
'A Practical Guide to Claims Arising from Fatal Accidents' by James Patience
'A Practical Approach to Clinical Negligence Post-Jackson' by Geoffrey Simpson-Scott
'A Practical Guide to Personal Injury Trusts' by Alan Robinson
'Occupiers, Highways and Defective Premises Claims: A Practical Guide Post-Jackson' by Andrew Mckie
'Employers' Liability Claims: A Practical Guide Post-Jackson' by Andrew Mckie
'A Practical Guide to Subtle Brain Injury Claims' by Pankaj Madan
'The Law of Driverless Cars: An Introduction' by Alex Glassbrook
'A Practical Guide to Costs in Personal Injury Cases' by Matthew Hoe
'A Practical Guide to Alternative Dispute Resolution in Personal Injury Claims –

Getting the Most Out of ADR Post-Jackson' by Peter Causton, Nichola Evans, James Arrowsmith
'A Practical Guide to Personal Injuries in Sport' by Adam Walker & Patricia Leonard
'A Practical Guide to Marketing for Lawyers' by Catherine Bailey & Jennet Ingram
'The No Nonsense Solicitors' Practice: A Guide To Running Your Firm' by Bettina Brueggemann
'Baby Steps: A Guide to Maternity Leave and Maternity Pay' by Leah Waller
'The Queen's Counsel Lawyer's Omnibus: 20 Years of Cartoons from the Times 1993-2013' by Alex Steuart Williams

These books and more are available to order online direct from the publisher at www.lawbriefpublishing.com, where you can also read free sample chapters. For any queries, contact us on 0844 587 2383 or mail@lawbriefpublishing.com.

Our books are also usually in stock at www.amazon.co.uk with free next day delivery for Prime members, and at good legal bookshops such as Hammicks and Wildy & Sons.

We are regularly launching new books in our series of practical day-to-day practitioners' guides. Visit our website and join our free newsletter to be kept informed and to receive special offers, free chapters, etc.

You can also follow us on Twitter at www.twitter.com/lawbriefpub.

INDEX

www.ingramcontent.com/pod-product-compliance
Lightning Source LLC
LaVergne TN
LVHW022048200926
848481LV00003B/828
9781911035664